MY LIFE AS A DOG

L. A. DAVENPORT

P-WAVE PRESS

CONTENTS

PART I
WATERLOO SUNSET

CHAPTER ONE

I AM AWAKE. I DON'T KNOW WHY AND, FOR A SECOND, I don't know where I am.

I am in bed, my bed. The faint traces of a dream float in the shadows and the slowly undulating folds of the curtains.

There it is again, that sensation – electric, almost ticklish, exquisitely unbearable – on my elbow. I look around and he is staring at me from his bed on the floor. His tail is wagging and his eyes are shining with nervousness and happiness. He licks his lips and swallows. I smile and he lies down, placing his chin flat on the edge of the bed and looking up at me.

I am fully awake now, and the day begins.

FIVE MINUTES LATER, we are outside. I am in yesterday's clothes, quickly dressed, unshowered, untidy hair hidden under a flat cap. I am unclean, unpresentable. But he is happy. His lead shakes as he skips along the street, his head up, proud, searching, then down again when he catches a scent. His black fur, patched in brown on his legs and around his chops, shines in the morning sun. I squint, then remember I have my sunglasses in my pocket.

As I put them on, he scuttles to a halt and crouches on his back paws, looking back at me over his shoulder. Perfect. *Please remember to have brought his shit bags.* The swift patting of pockets, and then the relief at finding that familiar plastic roll.

I am sweating slightly and the night before is tugging at me. *You have to go back to bed.* It was a late one. I tie up the bag, while he stares at me as if I'm the one who has done something wrong.

"Shall we go home?"

No response, no movement; just sad, put-upon eyes.

"C'mon, let's go home."

I tug at the lead. He resists, tipping his body away from me to counterbalance the force. He is low-down enough, and strong enough, that it can be hard to shift him when he is determined. And this morning, he is determined. He stares at me with defiant eyes and glances up the road in the opposite direction to our flat.

"You want to go up there? Today?"

He wags his tail. I know what he wants to do, but I pretend I don't understand.

"Let's go home, eh? I've got work to do."

I turn to leave and tug on the lead. He digs in and won't budge. When I turn back to him, he stares at me, then glances up the road and back at me. He looks a little nervous, but still determined. He is well aware that I could simply pick him up and carry him. But I like him knowing what he wants and expressing himself, and that occasionally means letting him do things even when I'm not very keen.

I check the time. I don't have much work and what I do have isn't urgent. No need to rush back.

"Okay then, have it your way."

4

I take a step forward. He wags his tail, waits until I take another step, and then scampers off up the hill until he reaches the end of his extendable lead and is catapulted backwards, as if on the end of a bungee cord.

We amble past Thornhill Square, one of his favourite haunts, but he doesn't want to go there today. We continue up Richmond Avenue, past all the mismatched Georgian and early Victorian townhouses. I say 'amble'. I am ambling. I am hungover and uncomfortable in my clothes and my skin, hoping I will see no one I know. He is scampering and careering about, left and right, up and back, checking every tree, chasing every squirrel regardless of whether he has any chance of catching it, and taking delight. Delight in the day, in the morning sun, in everything he comes across, in getting to do what he wants.

At the junction with Barnsbury Road, I decide to test his intentions. I think I know where he wants to go and what he wants to get out of the walk, but I am not so keen on going that way and would rather wander around the quiet backstreets and squares of Barnsbury. So, while he heads straight on, I turn left towards Thornhill Road and make the double-click sound with my mouth that says we are changing direction.

He stops and stares at me, already leaning against the pull of the lead in case I want to drag him away. I smile at him, and he relaxes and sits down.

"Where do you want to go?"

A half-wag of the tail and a slight bob of the head as he swallows. I know what he wants me to do.

"Okay then."

Letting the lead go slack, I walk around him in a circle, at first in the direction of home, and then carrying on until I reach the point between where he is sitting now and where he wants to go. As I arrive at that exact spot, he stands up and, wagging his tail, trots past me and continues along Richmond Avenue towards Upper Street. I smile to myself as I watch him, happy, skipping.

So you wanted to go that way all along, you old devil, even when we were down at the bottom of the hill.

We cross Liverpool Road by The Regent pub and head towards Milner Square. He knows the route by heart and runs ahead, around the corner and towards the alleyway leading to Almeida Street. I know what he's trying to do, so I pull him up and shorten his lead. He is extremely put out and tugs against the lead, his feet scrabbling on the pavement. He snakes around a dustbin and I pull him away from it. He stares back at me with an expression that says 'leave me alone', and then runs on into the alleyway.

As we head down Almeida Street towards Upper Street, I am somewhat dispirited to be out in this part of the world. Not only have I not showered, but I am also certainly not properly dressed to be among smart workers on their way to offices and boutiques, coffee in one hand, mobile phone in the other, shiny and bright and ready for their day. More than that, I know, from now until we turn away from Upper Street and head back home, I will be in an almost constant battle with him.

We pass the Almeida Theatre and I make a note, for the umpteenth time, to try to get tickets for the latest production, whatever it is. At the end of the road, he pulls right and dives along Upper Street. I lock his lead and hold him in check. When I round the corner, I find him splayed like a frog, trying not to be dragged backwards. A young woman in a business suit and with exceptionally neat hair and perfect make-up is staring at him, her glossy red mouth open in a cartoon smile.

"How adorable! What a beautiful dachshund!" She

gestures at him with her recycled board coffee cup and stares at me with melting eyes. I try to look remotely sophisticated, or at least not hopelessly dishevelled, and smile back.

"What's he called?"

"Kevin."

He looks back at me over his shoulder with a furrowed brow. He is still in full frog pose, straining against the lead.

"Kevin! That's hilarious! I love it."

"Yes, it's great until you have to shout it out in the park."

She laughs and stares at Kevin, her eyes wide with joy. I adjust my stance, but he takes it as the off and scrabbles furiously, desperate to get on our way.

"Well, I'll leave you boys to it. Have a lovely day, and lovely to meet you, Kevin."

He looks up at her with his huge black and brown saucer eyes and she turns to me, melting once more.

"Thank you. It seems he's pretty keen to get on today."

"I don't want to keep him from his duties." She laughs again. "Bye."

"Bye."

Kevin rushes on and I follow him, watching him as he runs, darts and dives. He is a maniac in a fur coat, a slithering black-and-tan eel, desperately seeking, never resting. He is hunting today, completely lost in the moment, in 1,000 smells that crowd him; trapped in a sensory prison in which he can see nor hear nothing other than the million-and-one scents that promise deliciousness, but are always so deliciously out of reach.

He is the archetypal scavenger; a consummate hunter; a nimrod, always on the lookout, nose just off the ground, relentlessly searching. He grabs and lungs, snaps and twists to get anything he can. He loves Upper

Street, with its tossed wrappers, discarded chicken bones, bin bags burst by greedy foxes and kitchen left-overs. He goes for anything and everything, no matter how grey and dirty the meat, no matter how bleached and dry the bone. It's not about hunger – he is well fed and in wonderful shape – it's the chase, especially when it's against me. He loves to dive for something, hoping he'll get there before I realise what is happening, then grab it and swallow it before I can take it off him.

When I first knew him, I didn't really know what I was doing and would let him eat stuff – and I use the generic catch-all term 'stuff' advisedly – if I hadn't been quick enough to stop him from getting it. But he has been sick so many times that I now try to fetch any-thing he has got out from his jaws before he can swallow it down. Consequently, if he does, on rare oc-casions, manage to sell me a dummy and get a bone or lump of what was presumably once meat into his mouth, he wolfs it down as quickly as possible so I have nothing to get hold of, and then trots off, satisfied and triumphant. Today, he is on sparkling form: an athlete on top of his game; an Olympic gymnast, leaving no paper, bag or leaf unturned in his quest to beat me to something, anything.

By the time we reach Berners Road and turn off Upper Street, I reckon I've got the better of him and he hasn't managed to get anything, despite numerous at-tempts along the way. It is a victory for me. Running the gauntlet of Upper Street is never easy, and it's rather disquieting to watch this loving and wonderful companion turned into an obsessive, possessed wild animal, intoxicated by the thrill of the chase and the scent in his nose and forgetting all else.

We go up Broomfield Street and pass The Angelic pub. As he snakes along the pavement, I am reminded of the time he dived behind a bin on Caledonian Road.

When he re-emerged, had an entire roast chicken in his mouth, so large that it obscured his face. He didn't really know what to do with this ultimate prize, this magical find, and when I told him to drop it, he did, unsure what else to do. It was only as I dragged him away that he realised what a terrible mistake he had made and scrabbled to get back to it, to no avail. The utter, complete disappointment was carved deeply into his brow.

AWAY FROM THE distractions of Upper Street, he calms down. His tail drops a little and his fur lies flat on his back. He lifts his head and looks around, once more happy with the world. I relax and enjoy the growing day, until I remember that I still haven't started my work.

When we get back home, he runs upstairs and is waiting for me at the door of the flat, staring at the lock, then at me, then at the lock, his tail wagging furiously. But something isn't right. Normally, he is so excited that he yawns with nervousness, but today his mouth is shut. He glances at me. I can see he is distracted. But why?

Oh, I know…

I reach down to his face and he tries to avoid my hand. I grab his head and run my hand along his jaw.

"You little devil."

There it is, on the right-hand side, tucked into his cheek: the telltale hard lump of a piece of bone. I must have missed him grabbing it while we were on Upper Street. Instead of swallowing it straight down, doubtless because it would have taken too long, he hid it in his cheek, hoping I wouldn't notice until he had got it inside and could hide it in his bed.

"You thought you could fool me, eh?"

I open his mouth and reach in, pulling out a sodden,

unidentifiable grey mass that was clearly once part of an animal.

"That's disgusting."

He stares at the bone, and then glares at me while I unlock the door and open it. He sits by the door, staring at my hand, knowing he'll never get his prize back, but not wanting to give it up quite yet.

I unclip his lead.

"Oh, go on, get inside."

He carries on staring at my hand. I move towards the door and he jumps ahead of me, all the while following every movement of my hand as I slam the door.

CHAPTER TWO

Inside, I throw away the bone and wash my hands, while he hurtles around the flat, running down the corridor, into the living room, around the coffee table, back up the corridor and screeching to a halt in front of me, panting, with legs splayed, eyes wide. Seeing I'm not yet ready, he does another circuit and stops again in front of the kitchen door, where the carpet ends.

He makes to run off again, but I grab him and take off his collar and clean his paws. He lifts each leg in turn for me, but doesn't look at me. He is staring into the kitchen, eyes fixed on an old plastic takeaway box under the sink. At the third paw, he thinks we're done and tries to run off. I grab him again and hold him while I clean the other back paw. He glances at me and, the very second I have finished, dashes into the kitchen. He stands next to the sink, pointing at the box with his nose, licking his lips, glancing up at me and then back at the box. I watch him and he lifts and places his two front paws in turn, like a horse from the Spanish Riding School in Vienna, all the while licking his lips. He glances at me again and, head shaking, huffs and puffs.

"I'm sorry, I haven't got any. I forgot to buy them."

He glances at me out of the corner of his eye and steps his paws more vigorously, his body shaking with the concentrated effort.

"Sorry. We've run out."

He stares at me and barks.

"Don't bark at me."

He barks again, and then runs around the flat. He grabs at a toy from the wooden box by his bed as he passes, misses, goes back for it, gets angry and flings it away. He runs up to me, stares at the box under the sink, and then back at me.

"I know. I'm sorry. I'll get some more later. I promise."

I grab his bowl and fill it up with his food.

"Here, have this instead."

I put it down and change his water. He looks hopefully into his food bowl, and then up at me again.

"It's your breakfast. You like that."

He sticks his nose in, grabs a mouthful of kibbles and walks over to the hall carpet. He scatters the small brown pellets on the floor and first sniffs them, then eats them one by one before trotting back to repeat the exercise. When he has eaten about half the bowlful, he heads to the living room, without looking back. Relieved that the crisis is over, I make a mental note to buy some chew sticks when we go out for a walk later.

By the time I sit down at my desk and start my computer, he is sitting on his bed, staring at me and wagging his tail, his toys scattered around in front of him on the floor. He is clearly brimming over with energy and will need to go for a long walk to burn it off.

I check my email. Not too many messages. I have only one article to write today. Maybe we could go out for the afternoon, if nothing else comes in. As I settle down to work, I can hear him huffing and straining to do something.

I turn and watch as he slowly folds himself under his blanket. With each quarter turn, he tucks the blanket under himself, drops his rump on to it to hold it in place, then turns another quarter, tucks the blanket under him and holds it down with his rump, repeating until he is completely cocooned by his blanket, his body bent into a perfect circle underneath the dark material. He sighs deeply, and then slightly extracts his head to leave his nose sticking out and one beady eye trained on me.

I smile at him and turn back to the computer. He sighs deeply once more, and then falls asleep, his breath rasping against the edge of the blanket lying loosely over his nostrils. He does not sleep deeply, however. As soon as I finish my work, I lean back slightly and breathe in. Instantly he is awake, sitting up on his hind legs and wagging his tail, his eyes glistening.

I stare at him.

"How do you know, eh?"

He wags his tail even harder, licks his lips and swallows.

"Okay then."

I push back my chair and lean forward. He jumps forward and places his nose on my foot, then runs down the hall towards the kitchen. When I arrive, he plants himself next to where his lead and harness hang and bounces up and down on his front paws, making his ears flap and looking like an overexcited elephant.

"Hold on. Hold on!"

I look in the fridge and grab a couple of carrots and radishes. Taking his water bottle, I fill it up. I leave the kitchen to get a blanket and a bag and march down the hall. Panicking, he follows me, putting his nose over my foot with each step to undo imaginary shoe laces – I am wearing only socks, but he makes the point just the same. When he sees I am going for a bag, he runs back

13

to the kitchen, takes his lead off the hook, places it on the floor in the middle of the hall, lies down behind it and stares up at me with his head on his paws.

"Don't worry, you're coming too."

He stands up and stares down at the lead. He can barely contain himself while I click him into his harness and attach his lead. I take some shit bags and another blanket just in case, and we are off, him clattering down the stairs, then bouncing from step to step, then jumping to the bottom from the highest step he can manage, before running straight to the door. I always wince when he jumps the last part of the stairs as he once dislocated his shoulder, but I let him do it because I assume that me clumsily trying to stop him in mid-air will only make things worse.

Outside, I don't know which way we should go, and we stand on the street corner, him assuming we will go in one direction and leaning against the pull of the lead, me looking up and down the road, searching for some kind of inspiration. We have the afternoon ahead of us, and there is so much to see and do.

Once I have decided on our direction, he trots ahead of me, paying no attention to me. He is back on the hunt, not as manically as earlier, but still scavenging for whatever he can find, with head down and tail quivering like an antenna.

We head across Pentonville Road and into Finsbury. I am thinking about which route to take across Clerkenwell or whether simply to head straight down Rosebery Avenue when a dog appears from nowhere and lunges at Kevin. I use his lead to spin him around in a circle away from the dog's jaws and flip him up into my arms.

Initially confused, the other dog, which I now realise is an extremely muscular and grim-looking English bulldog, regains its composure and leaps up as high

14

as it can to bite Kevin, who swings his rump out of the way of the snapping jaws. Undeterred, the bulldog then climbs my leg, paw over paw, snapping all the way as I lift Kevin higher and higher to keep him out of reach. I am shouting at the bulldog to get down and trying to shake it off, but it doesn't heed me, and I realise that I can't hit it or push it off because that would mean having to let go of Kevin.

After an eternity, the bulldog's owner appears from around a corner. She runs over and smacks it with the end of its lead and shouts at it to get down. It regards her with disdain out of the corner of its eye, and then slowly, reluctantly eases itself down my body, once again paw over paw. I am shocked, and Kevin is shaking with fright.

"I'm so sorry," the woman says.

"You should keep that thing on a lead. It's dangerous."

"No, no, he's a lovely boy. He only wants to play."

I stare at her and fix her in the eye. "Don't be ridiculous. It was trying to bite my dog, at the very least, and Kevin wouldn't have stood a chance."

Ashamed, she turns away from me. I walk off and, when I look back, I see she has attached the bulldog's lead and is trying to drag it off. But it stands there and stares at us with hate in its eyes.

CHAPTER THREE

WHEN I PUT KEVIN BACK DOWN ON THE PAVEMENT, HE runs off at full speed and angrily chases after a crisp packet. He carries on down the road, and then stops. He wees on a lamppost, but he is concentrating on something else. His head is up and his tail is a stiff cable, quivering with the force of his laser stare.

I follow his eyes and spot two squirrels playing at the foot of a tree on the other side of the road. They are scampering back and forth, seemingly without any purpose. As soon as Kevin notices me take a step forward, he flings himself into the road and I have to stop him running straight into the line of traffic. As I hold him steady and then drag him back from the edge of the pavement, he yelps and barks, desperate to go after the squirrels – his hated enemies, tied only with cats in the league of despicableness.

I have to drag Kevin down the road for at least 100 yards before he finally stops trying to chase the squirrels, now long gone from the bottom of the tree, and gets back to earnest scavenging. Even without the traffic, I couldn't let him have his head, even for the smallest of chases. On a late night wandering around Barnsbury, I watched him shoot under a parked van. I didn't bother too much until I heard a screech and a cat shot out the other side. Kevin emerged a few seconds later with a triumphant look on his face and a beard of cat fur.

HE GIVES up on his relentless scavenging only when we turn away from the main road and its fast-food outlets. We follow backstreets and cross hidden parks, and his pace slackens. He looks around, he wags his tail, he skips. He is enjoying himself and the world around him.

As we cross a garden square, resplendent in autumn colours, he spots some office workers having an impromptu picnic and runs over to see what he can beg. They laugh at his demented enthusiasm, and his obvious desperation to go over to them. Then he spots a dog, smaller than the bulldog, and his mood changes. He falls quiet and levels his head with his shoulders. The fur on the back of his neck stands up and he runs purposefully, directly at the dog. I know what's coming and I pull him in before he can reach it. The other dog is initially pleased to see Kevin, but then stops wagging its tail and seems confused when it sees Kevin's attitude.

After another skirmish with two more squirrels, we leave the square and head towards Bloomsbury. As we are approaching Russell Square, Kevin begins whining and almost howling in pain. There seems to be nothing wrong with him, but then I remember the last time this happened and realise we must be near...

He shoots forward and I spin around to see two magnificent police horses and their riders.

I step back and try to drag him with me, but he has completely lost himself. Intoxicated by the heady equine smell, he is in pure hunt mode. He howls and yelps and barks as he strains with all his might to get to them. I apologise, clearly with a look of acute shame on my face. Both riders and horses look down on tiny Kevin, ridiculous and clearly lost to sanity, with what can only be described as bemused disdain. All four of them are somewhat inscrutable, but I shudder to think what could have happened if his lead had snapped and he had been able to get at them.

When we finally reach Russell Square, I can see he is getting tired. He didn't eat much breakfast and he has been going hell for leather ever since we left, not to mention it being a warm day. He is enjoying the grass under his feet and skips every now and again. I check my watch. It's a good time to stop. We've been going for at least 45 minutes, and if he gets much more tired I'll have to carry him, which I am in no mood to do.

I pick a spot in the shade, away from everyone else. When I drop the bag on the floor, he immediately sticks his head fully inside it.

"Eh, eh! Hold on."

I push him back and he sits down. He watches me expectantly as I pull out a blanket and shake it out. Before I can finish laying it out, he clambers on top, sitting on his hind legs like a side-saddle horse rider and looking around for whatever can be seen. I fill his portable bowl with water and he quickly drinks down as much as he can before returning to his lookout.

He glances at me when I take out a carrot and wipe it clean. When I bite the ends off, he comes over and sits down in front of me, wagging his tail and licking his lips. I offer him the top and he gently takes it from my hand and carries it just off the blanket so he can crunch it in peace. Despite eating, he watches me out of the corner of his eye as I take a couple of bites. Once he's finished, he comes back, staring at the carrot and licking his lips. I give him the tail and he repeats the process.

The second time he comes back, he watches me like a hawk and, when I bite off a piece that's clearly for him, he lunges for it.

"Wait!"

He checks himself and sits back down, staring at the carrot, but glancing at me. I slowly proffer the carrot piece and he waits until it is almost touching his lips before he takes it gently from my hand.

"Good boy."

I finish the carrot and, once he has wolfed down his piece, he comes back for another.

"Sorry, all gone."

He looks in my hands, pushing his nose into my palms. I pull back my hands and show him they are empty.

"Look, nothing. Sorry."

He sits back down, then, remembering the bag, ambles over to it. I pull out a couple of radishes. He wags his tail and waits while I bite off the top and bottom of both of them. I put the four ends on the blanket and he picks them up, takes them over to the other side and eats them one by one.

I lie down on the blanket and open my arm. He walks into the crook, turns and sits on his hind legs so that his rump is pressed into my armpit and his side is leaning against my ribcage, and then resumes his lookout.

I think about falling asleep and a wave of tiredness sweeps over me. It's been a long week. I start to drift away, then remember that he could run off if he sees a dog or a cat, or could be attacked, so I force myself to stay awake.

The fountains in the middle of the square are on today and I can hear children frolicking in the jets of water, their excited squeals drifting through the rumble of endless traffic. Kevin is watching some pigeons searching in the nearby grass. I know he will never go for them, unless they are very close. He spots a squirrel being fed by a local resident at a nearby bench. He yelps and barks a little, so I place my hand on his barrel chest and squeeze him towards me. He licks his lips and relaxes a little.

I watch two students lazing on the grass and remember when I was studying in the gardens of my college, I and a friend lying on the grass with our folders and notepads, pretending to learn. A family of ducks from the pond were wandering about on the grass. A duckling spotted us and waddled over, followed by the mother and the rest of the brood. Fascinated, the ducklings came right up to us. They tugged at our papers and pulled at my trousers. Two adventurous ducklings even clambered, slipping and sliding all the way, on to my boots and made their way up my legs. Their mother watched, letting them carry on, but keeping an eye on them, and on me. I tried to stay still and quiet, but the ducklings tickled me as they scrabbled on my trousers. I laughed. Startled, they jumped off and the family moved on to search elsewhere for food in the grass.

I look at Kevin, now calm and uninterested in pigeons and squirrels. He rests his head on my arm and his entire body relaxes.

"I wish you'd been there."

He flicks up his ears to listen, but decides whatever I said doesn't require his attention. What fun life would have been at university if he had been with me. But then I realise that he would have attacked the ducklings and I'm glad he wasn't there.

CHAPTER FOUR

We walk a little aimlessly towards Covent Garden. I can't decide where I want to go. I mean, of course, I am walking aimlessly. Kevin is full of purpose, launching himself from one side of the pavement to the other as he scavenges for food, drawn by every single smell and hint at hidden treasure. The calm of the park is gone now, although he is not as obsessed or manic as he was on Upper Street.

I had fancied a wander into a clothes shop or two, but the hot confusion of a dog with too much energy can be a little overwhelming in the confines of the aisles. Instead, I step away from the main streets and head to some less well-trodden paths. To much protest, I drag him away from Shaftesbury Avenue and up to St Giles in the Fields. He weaves around the bins and dropped food cartons and the legs of startled office works, surprised out of their smartphone reverie by the scuttling sliver of black-and-tan energy by their feet.

In Phoenix Gardens, he slows to a trot, lifts his head and wags his tail as he steps on to the grass and into the sunshine. He surveys the scene happily, then immediately runs towards a couple sitting on the grass having, he evidently assumes, a picnic. As I stop the lead from extending any further, he bounces off the end, then runs in a circle like a horse on a training ground, happily bounding through the uncut grass.

From there, we cross Shaftesbury Avenue and head down Mercer Street. He wanders up to Stringfellows as we pass, caught by a smell emanating from under the door. At the junction with Long Acre, a homeless man tries to stroke him as we pass, but he ducks underneath the outstretched hand and carries on, head pointing forward in a manner reminiscent of a Victorian explorer.

On and on, and down St Martin's Lane, neither looking left nor right. Even some dropped food and a pile of newspapers don't interest him. At William IV Street, he takes a sharp left and heads straight along the road. I glance across the road and remember an evening out with friends in a pub that no longer exists, realising I am far happier now than I ever was then.

He turns left again up Chandos Place. Hunger creeps up on me and, as we pass a small Thai restaurant, I decide to stop for lunch. Much to his disappointment, I halt his determined progress. Legs splayed, he looks at me over his shoulder with unconcealed frustration. I walk up to the door of the restaurant and he glances at it before straightening up and trotting after me.

We take a table outside and I drape his blanket over my knee so that he can sit on my lap. He stands up on my legs and places his head on my shoulder so he can look through the restaurant window. The waitress looks a little surprised when she brings out the menus and sees him perched on my lap. I want to explain that he can't be left on the floor as he gets so angry at other dogs and, anyway, he feels the cold very quickly and will soon be shivering, but I simply smile and thank her for the menus.

We are alone, sitting outside. He tries to get between me and the menu to have my undivided attention, but then becomes bored and lies down, his back legs folded to stop himself slipping off my lap and his head and forepaws dangling over the side of my thighs. He stares at the floor and his throat is pressed against my leg, so that every lick of the lips and swallow is transmitted directly to me. I imagine it cannot be comfortable to lie like that, but I suppose that, if it really bothered him, he would change position.

I order, and then forget what I asked for as soon as the waitress departs. I look up and down the empty road. I think about texting a friend who works nearby, but decide against it. After a few minutes, I realise I am anxious and distracted. Yet another of my clients, and thus another source of income, has gone bust.

Since the financial crash, I have lost all but one of my clients, and even they seem to have less and less work for me. From having a sense of general security and comfort with my life just a few months ago, I am slowly being pushed to the edge. I don't know how much longer I can carry on being freelance. I have already stopped as many monthly expenses as I can and have spent what meagre savings I had. If things don't pick up soon, I will be destitute.

I could try to get a job, but that could take months, even if I did find something suitable, and there is precious little temporary work available. Even if I find an in-house version of what I already do freelance, the reason I have so little work is because there is no work, so no one is hiring. I could, of course, go to my family, cap in hand, for a temporary bailout but, if things don't improve, temporary could quickly become permanent and I will have to think of something drastic.

But what else could I do? I think back to my first job after university, selling suits for Jaeger on Regent

Street. It was a blissful, simple and oddly fulfilling part of my life. Blissful because, after several years of studying at university and all the pressures that entails, I was helping people with a pleasant and sometimes joyous part of their lives – to choose a piece of clothing that, by its very design, is intended to make them feel good. It was simple because, well, the only concerns I had at the time were whether there was enough stock and custom, and dealing with the sticky issue of who would earn the commission from a sale. It was oddly fulfilling as I learned I had a talent, hitherto unknown, for selling in a shop. I enjoyed talking to customers, making them feel comfortable with buying what they wanted, and maintaining the floor.

During a more unfortunate moment in my life, I tried selling advertising space in trade magazines to small-to-medium businesses in Europe. This was during my early days after having arrived in London. The company was based in an anaemic neon-lit office and was full of wide boys. I had been told that, every time I got someone on the phone, I was to stand up and shout the pre-prepared pitch as that was the only way the person on the other end would get excited about the idea. We were given the directories of companies that had attended trade fairs for ice cream manufacturers and the like and told only to call businesses in non-English speaking countries, as whoever answered the phone would not have enough command of the language to question the product. I managed four days, rang in sick on the Friday and quit on the Monday.

In comparison, selling suits to young men due to get married or businessmen wanting to spruce up their image was a joy. It was also a time in my life when I had almost no responsibilities and was intoxicated with getting to know London. But could I go back to that now? Surely not. I don't even know if the shop is still open.

KEVIN SWALLOWS and shifts on my lap. A tourist couple walks past. Where are they from? America? I look down at the dog and sigh. No, I couldn't go back to that life, even if I wanted to. I don't have anyone to look after Kevin during the day.

So what else? I wrack my brains and my mind drifts back to the narrow terraced house of my grandparents. While Grandad slipped into a diabetic half-world, taking their greedy, overweight Labrador with him, Grandma turned socks for the local factory to supplement their retirement. Clear plastic bags full of cheap sports socks littered the house every time I visited. It didn't strike me at the time, being only eleven, but the factory bosses had calculated that it was cheaper and easier to send their socks by the bagful to be paired by retired ladies in the surrounding streets than to buy a machine to do it. Every week, they would take away bags full of paired socks, then replace them with the next batch. My aunt had worked in knitwear in Leicester too, although no more. Generation after generation, giving the best of their lives to an industry now long gone. Who lives in that terraced house now? Where do they work, if they have any work?

I remember walking along the old railway tracks with Grandad and his lumbering, panting dog. The rails were gone, but the steep banking that hid the belching, rumbling trains from the neighbouring houses was still there. I wanted to run up the bank, to test myself, but I didn't want to leave Grandad. He always wanted to tell me things about his life: how he had installed the electricity supply to the area; how things were before the modern world came along, with its televisions and conveniences.

One day, he told me that he was getting tired and might not be able to walk along the old railway tracks with me anymore. I asked him if he would mind if I ran up the banking. No, no, go on, he said, and I ran as hard as I could across the grass to give myself some momentum once I hit the slope.

I climbed and I climbed. It was much harder than I'd thought it would be, but I didn't want to give up. I would never get the chance to do this again. Almost at the top, I realised I didn't want it to stop; I didn't want to reach the destination and the journey to be over. So I stopped climbing and turned around, planting my feet in the weeds and the white flowers so I wouldn't slip back down. I looked out over the red brickscape of Leicester, and then down at Grandad and his dog. They seemed so small from up there. I called out to him and he stopped and waved, and then walked on.

THE WAITRESS APPEARS with my spring rolls. The weather has turned and they steam hot in the breeze. Kevin is immediately interested and stretches as he stands up on my lap to see what has arrived that smells so fascinating. The waitress looks nervous and avoids his inquisitive nose, sniffing the air enthusiastically. I force his head to one side and smile at the waitress. She smiles back awkwardly.

"They're not for you, eh," I say to him.

He glances at me out of the corner of his eye, but still strains to get a better look at the spring rolls.

"Enjoy," the waitress says, and then leaves.

I gaze at the plate. The rolls still look hot and I wait for them to cool. It's getting cold and I wish I had brought a coat for Kevin.

After a full minute of trying to get to the spring rolls, he finally gives up and settles down, resuming his casual drape across my lap. I pick up the first spring roll and hold it delicately, blowing on the end. I think back to my lack of work. What am I going to do? I can't go on like this. I'll end up broke and on the street at this rate.

I lean forward to take a bite, but something catches my eye. At the other end, Kevin has put his mouth around the spring roll, also to take a bite. He looks up at me, his eyes wide.

"Hey, what are you doing? That's mine."

Slowly he opens his mouth and, licking his lips guilty, lies back down on my lap. I consider eating the rest of the spring roll, but I think about his slobber on the other end and put it down.

And then I laugh.

CHAPTER FIVE

A WHILE LATER, AS THE DAY FADES TO EVENING, WE FIND ourselves on South Bank, Kevin trotting quietly beside me as we head towards Lambeth Palace and away from the tourists. He is tiring and keeps looking up at me as if to check whether we will continue or go back home.

At an unremarkable spot on the pavement, he comes to an abrupt halt and sits down, looking up at me imploringly. I know what this means. I stand and watch him for a moment.

"Do you want some carrot?"

He wags his tail a little and steps towards me, head down, nose to my shoes. I pull a carrot from my bag and bite a piece off for him, which he eats slowly, watching the joggers and tourists pass. Another piece, eaten even more slowly.

When he has finished, I give him a drink of water. Sated, he stands next to me and looks up into my eyes, wagging his tail. He lifts his front paws off the floor, as if to jump up at me, and lets them drop. He wants me to pick him up.

I lift him into my arms. He folds his legs into the crook of my elbow and lays his body along my forearm. He tucks his forepaws into the palm of my hand and licks his lips contentedly. I put my fingers into the spaces between his pads. His feet are hot and dusty from the miles and miles he has walked on his tiny legs. He needed a walk, a long one, to burn off his excess energy, and I know he will be peaceful now for the next few days.

"Shall we go home?"

He wags his tail and leans over to lick my face. I try to pull away, but can't reach far enough and he gets my cheek, licking it comprehensively.

I turn and walk towards Waterloo Station and he settles into position, me watching the sunset slowly grow across the sky and him following every smell with his nose as we pass food stalls and passers-by with hot drinks. I ponder which route to take back to Islington and I'm grateful that it's not too hot to carry him.

For a change, I opt for the Waterloo and City line to Bank, so we can catch the Northern Line up to Angel. I normally love the quirkiness of this line, with its single stop and single purpose underlining the predictability of the commuter life – at least as it was when the line was built. But we have arrived during rush hour, and it takes an age to get on to a train and trundle off to Bank. My arm is already tired and I am frustrated with the City workers, their heads down, catching no one's eye. Hardly anyone notices that I am carrying a dog – very unusual on this line and in this part of town – and I am both amused and saddened that there is so little interaction, with everyone trapped in their lonely tunnel, enslaved to the pursuit of wealth and status.

I used to feel the same. One of the reasons I left Jaeger and the genteel world of suit selling was because I wanted a career; to be a success; to live up to the expectations of my peers and realise the promise of my scholastic achievements. What would be the point of going to a university like Cambridge, so the argument went, if I wasn't to then go on to be the best in my chosen field? I didn't need a degree from Cambridge to tell a man what shirt would go with a houndstooth jacket, did I?

Perhaps what I loved about that time was being able to step away from the endless competition and alleviate the pressure. I had gone to university to become a doctor, but had realised it was not for me and had eventually switched to social anthropology. But once I left university, I had no idea what I wanted to do with my life. Secretly, I wanted to be a journalist and a writer, but that seemed impossible, given I had studied science, not English, and I knew no one in that world.

Eventually, I recognised I couldn't sell suits to middle-aged men forever. I wanted more from life. I had ambitions. I wanted to test myself and to do something that would last. But what? I settled on publishing, with the reason being that it would be an education in writing to work on others' words.

It turned out, however, that I was not very good at being an office worker. I found the structure and narrowness of expectations oppressive. Rather than prosper, I wilted, but it took a good long while to pluck up the courage to go freelance. In the end, it was the draw of being able to spend more time with Kevin that had been the clincher. With his joy or anger, his contentedness or frustration, his tiredness or energy, he is always immediate, always present. He exists only in the here and now. The rest he lets go, aside from the traces of memories and learned experiences. I wanted to be exposed to that all day, every day, to remind me to live now, not in hope for the future.

When the opportunity came up to leave the office and do the same work as a freelancer from home, I leapt at it. And now, on this train, surveying the bowed heads and furrowed brows, I am glad.

WHEN THE TRAIN arrives at Bank, the platform is already full, and our exodus only adds to the swell of people filling the tubes. Every corridor, hall and platform is lined with gently undulating rows of people, pretending it is normal to be massed like this, waiting patiently, quietly, to move forward. Conversations, where they are undertaken, are hushed and discreet. We inch forward, step by step, and time crawls to a standstill.

Kevin, on the other hand, is bright and alert, and loving every second. Perched on my tired arm, he is fascinated by the people and the smells. His nose is bobbing up and down constantly as he samples the air over and over. There are so many people here that it would be impossible to put such a small dog on the ground, even though I can see he has recovered from his earlier tiredness and is raring to go.

On and on we plod, step by step, inching down the platform. We turn into a narrow, short corridor leading to the main hallway. I can see the sign to the Northern Line in the distance and people striding purposefully by. As soon as we get through here, we'll be able to make quick progress. I am ready, just waiting for a chance to break through the crowd.

Out of the corner of my eye, but too late to stop him, I see Kevin lean forward and stick his nose fully into the ear of a woman by my side. She squeals and leaps sideways into the crowd, and is caught by a shocked businessman. Embarrassed, yet far too amused to communicate any remote degree of remorse, I push through the crowd to the main hallway. Kevin has his head wrapped around my neck to watch the mêlée he has caused, and I can hear his victim in the background.

"Oh gosh, I'm so sorry. I don't know what happened."

We turn and head towards the Northern Line and I squeeze him in my arms. He licks his lips and lays his head down on his paws.

CHAPTER SIX

WHEN WE ARRIVE BACK HOME, I REMEMBER, JUST AS I AM about to open the door, that I forgot to buy Kevin's chew sticks. I contemplate not buying them as we'll have to go out again. Can I be bothered? He is looking from the lock to me and back again, waiting for me to open the door. He is frantic, I realise, because he knows he didn't get a chew stick that morning and will run straight to the box, demanding one now. More frustration, more running around, and then I will have to go through the whole process again tomorrow morning.

"Come on, we're going to have to go back out again."

He stares at me, puzzled, and then glances at the door lock.

"I need to go to the shop to buy some chew sticks."

I head downstairs and he happily follows me, bouncing down each step. We go across the road to the corner shop and I carry him inside. He searches along the shelves, luxuriating in the symphony of smells, getting more excited as we reach the pet food section. By the time we find his chew sticks, his tail is wagging so hard that it's slapping the back of my jacket.

We pay and the young man behind the counter looks suspiciously at Kevin. The dog is at the same level as the chocolate bars by the till, but the man doesn't realise that Kevin's obsession with chew sticks is so great that it completely overwhelms all other desires.

Curiously, he only ever wants one per day, in the morning, but he must have that one. I wonder, not for the first time, what could be in them that makes him so addicted. Other dog owners tell me that their dogs are just as obsessed. He used to eat all sorts of treats, from all sorts of people, but he has gradually lost his taste for those. Now he only ever wants his chew stick, and only from me. In some ways, I'm quite happy that he is so uninterested in other things, but then again, what are those chew sticks doing to his body and mind?

Back again at the front door, he is calmer this time and waits patiently for me to get my keys out before trotting happily into the flat. In the hallway, he lies down on the carpet, waiting for me to clean his paws. When we are done, he slowly pulls himself to his feet, trots into the kitchen and stands by the treat box. As I open the packet, he starts jumping up and down on his forepaws and half barks at me.

I cut one in half and proffer it to him.

"Here you go."

He takes it gingerly from my hand and ambles out into the hallway to break it up into small pieces before wolfing them down one by one, all the while keeping an eye on me. By the time he comes back, I've boxed up the rest of the packet and put out his food, to which he pays scant interest. He sniffs around the kitchen while I start to prepare my dinner. Deciding I'm making nothing of interest, he trots off down the hall and into the living room.

While I chop the vegetables, I hear him playing with

his toys and moving his bed around. Before I start cooking, I go to the living room to put on some music and check on him. He is standing in the middle of his bed, bolt upright, wagging his tail and staring at me intently. His blanket is lying in a heap on the floor by his bed and there are dog toys everywhere.

"Do you want me to put your blanket over you? Is that it?"

He wags his tail vigorously.

"Okay then."

I pick up the blanket and go to drape it over him. He turns and drops down into the bed in a perfect circle, ready for the blanket. I lay it over him and I can hear him lick his lips. The material rises and falls as he breathes deeply, and then gives a contented sigh. I think about putting all his toys away, but I can't be bothered and put a record on instead before heading back to the kitchen and leaving him alone.

When dinner is ready to be eaten, I check my emails and see I've received a couple to do with potential jobs. Getting drawn into work, I end up eating at my desk. I am aware that Kevin is staring at me from under his blanket with one beady eye and can imagine what is going through his mind. It is sometimes disconcerting to be constantly watched like this.

I know he is completely fine with other people, being so sociable and communicative, and I have been told that he is perfectly happy staying with friends when I am away, but when I am with him, I am the sole focus of his attention. Almost everything he does is filtered through me, and it sometimes seems as if we are merging into one being. Our lives are symbiotic and we communicate very deeply. He has become more and more expressive, especially since my marriage ended and we started living alone together, and we have learned each other's personalities and ways to a profound level.

I FORGET about all this while I deal with the consequences of a work email, but at some point I become aware that Kevin is standing by my side, staring up at me and wagging his tail. I look down at him and he barks, still wagging his tail. I check the clock on my computer. It's 8pm. Of course, it's sofa time. I finish off an email, and he stays by my side. After a minute, he barks again and wags his tail.

"All right, all right. I'm coming."

As I send my email and push back from the desk, he gets up and wanders over to the sofa. He stands beside it, waiting for me. Only when I sit down does he jump on and walk into the crook of my arm. I turn on the TV and lie down. He doesn't immediately settle, but stands in front of my face, wagging his tail and blocking my view. He tries to lick my ear and I pull him away, folding his forelegs so he is forced to lie beside me, leaning against my side.

I flick through the channels while he finally lays his head down and licks his lips. I decide on a film I have already seen but that fits my mood. He sighs and settles even further into my arm, absentmindedly licking his forepaws, then my arm, and then his forepaws. After a few seconds, the licking becomes incredibly ticklish and irritating and I again pull his head away. He doesn't want to stop. I know he does it to be affectionate, but sometimes I cannot bear it. After half a minute of me holding his head away, he gives up and lies peacefully while I watch the film.

I MUST HAVE FALLEN asleep as I wake up to the sound of

a bark. Kevin is standing on the floor by the sofa, staring up at me and wagging his tail. I check the time, although I don't need to. It's 11.30pm. It's the same every day: first he escorts me to the sofa at 8pm for a lie down together; and then to bed at 11.30pm.

Still groggy, I pull myself off the sofa and he watches me, stepping out of the way and following me as I head to the hall, all the while wagging his tail.

"Time for the last wee of the day, then."

He meekly follows me and I put on his collar. Outside, it's cold and windy now, and we both smart as the cosy warmth of the living room is blown from us. He is in no mood to explore the possibilities of the night and wanders up to the first lamppost. Checking that I have seen him wee, he then runs back to the flat, bouncing off the end of the lead as we go. He doesn't wait for me to clean my teeth and takes himself straight to his bed next to mine, turning and turning in his blanket until he is completely cocooned.

When I get to bed, he is lost from view, only the rise and fall of his blanket betraying his presence. I watch him for a moment, and then read a few pages of my book, before turning out the light. In the darkness, I hear him lick his lips and sigh deeply.

I think back over the day. I remember the bulldog and it climbing up me to get at Kevin. Why does he get attacked so much by other dogs? And it's not just dogs that seem to have it in for him. For a period, we encountered a group of sixteen- or seventeen-year-olds on our morning and early evening walks. At first, when they saw Kevin, they would jeer at him and compare him unfavourably with a 'real' dog. It didn't happen very often and I didn't bother about it. After all, it was just some kids, and who cares what someone thinks about your dog?

Then it became more and more frequent, and the

insults and shouting became more and more intense and closer to us as we walked. It was a difficult situation as there were always five or six of them, all big lads, and infrequently they caught me off guard. Trying to react in a serious manner to make them stop would not only have left me in a potentially vulnerable position, but would also have put Kevin in danger. I tried to ignore it, but it became something I thought about every time I left the house, and Kevin became increasingly scared and jittery as he walked down that stretch of Caledonian Road.

One day, it reached a head. We turned the corner and they were there, lounging around outside the fried chicken shop. As soon as they saw us, they jeered at the dog and two of them bent down to shout in his face. Through gritted teeth, I walked past and Kevin kept his head down and forged on, completely ignoring them but obviously shaken. Afterwards, once we were out of sight, I stopped to gather myself. I looked at Kevin, who was staring back at me.

This is intolerable. It can't go on. Where will it end? They're getting worse and worse and evidently feel they have licence to act as they please. But what to do?

"Well, for one thing, we can't stand around here all day. We have to go home at some point."

Kevin continued to look back at me, a furrow on his brow.

I thought about all the options. They were just teenagers, but teenagers all the same. They needed to be reminded of some life lessons and how to behave, but not in such a way that the situation could get out of hand.

As I glanced up and down the street, wondering if they were still around, I noticed a placard tied to a lamppost. What was that?

Oh yes, it's polling day today. It's the general election. I really should have listened to the radio this morning.

Determined not to be intimidated, especially on a day when I got to exercise my democratic rights, I took Kevin back home, resolving that the situation with the teenagers was going to stop today. As we passed them on our way home, it was the same thing: shouting insults and bawling in the dog's face, and then laughter once we'd passed.

Leaving Kevin standing bemused in the middle of the living room, I marched straight back out again with my polling card. As I crossed the road to the local school, I saw the teenagers were still there, five or six of them chatting and laughing. After voting, I marched straight up to the gang. They realised who I was and stepped back a little. I walked up to their leader and stood a millimetre from his face, staring straight into his eyes.

"I'm s-s-sorry, mate. We didn't mean to hurt your dog. It's just a bit of fun."

"It's fun to you, maybe. But it isn't to us, especially not to him. He's a small dog and vulnerable, and you're scaring him, shouting at him like that."

"I'm sorry."

"The thing you don't realise is he came from a very bad home, where he was beaten and never taken out. He was abused, and he deserves a decent, quiet life."

"I promise we won't do it again. We was just having a laugh, you know?"

I stepped back and took him in. I could see the other teenagers standing around us out of the corner of my eye, unsure what to do.

"Okay then."

I stretched out my hand and we shook.

"Never again, then."

"I promise."

I nodded my head and left, only later thinking of the myriad other ways that situation could have played out.

BACK IN THE shadows of our bedroom, I listen to Kevin's slow and rhythmic breathing. I want to stroke him, but I don't want to wake him up, so I just listen. And then I fall asleep.

PART II
DANCE, DANCE, DANCE

CHAPTER SEVEN

MONTHS LATER, IN A FRIEND'S OFFICE, I notice out of the corner of my eye that Kevin is standing in the middle of the floor, staring at me. I am here to work on a script that a friend and I hope will eventually be made into a film. I wanted to bring him with me as I'd had a couple of days without him constantly by my side. He had seemed tired and not quite as enthusiastic about everything, and had only made a show of being bothered whenever I left. So I left him at home to rest.

This morning, however, I couldn't contemplate him not coming with me and, fortunately, he had run around the flat when I started to get ready and grabbed his lead from its hook and dropped it on to the middle of the floor in the hall. Of course he could come with me.

When we arrived, he had run around the whole workspace, bounding into each office, scurrying around the desks and chairs, and then back out and into the next one. Everyone laughed to see him and he pretended we were all playing a game of catch, with him 'it'. He ran right up to people, pressed himself on to the floor, stared up at them with mouth open and wide eyes, and then pelted away as soon as they bent down towards him. It was ridiculous and charming. Most people there didn't know him and were amazed by his boundless energy and enthusiasm.

Then I'd called his name and he ran after me into my friend's office. He stood in the middle of the floor and wagged his tail furiously, a look of absolute attention on his face.

"This is it. We're here."

He stared at me, still wagging his tail. I took out his blanket and laid it on the floor. He watched me doing it, and then resumed staring at me and wagging his tail. I patted the blanket.

"Here you go. This is for you."

He looked at me dubiously, and then walked on to the blanket, standing up straight and wagging his tail.

"This is it. This is what we came here for."

He sat down on his hind legs and stared at me, obviously unwilling or unable to relax and lie down. My friend laughed, and then we got on with writing.

After a while, I noticed Kevin had sat fully down, and then later curled himself up into a circle. We carried on with the scene we were tackling, trying to figure out how to fill a hole in the plot that had only just become apparent.

At first, we thought we could get away with ignoring it, but we soon realised that, if we could see it, then anyone else could. Not that plot holes are so rare in cinema, I pointed out. But, my friend reasoned, there is so much more scrutiny of a script from 'unknowns'. If you have a proven track record, then you will possibly get a script made, even if it's bad, whereas a script from an unknown has to be near-perfect even to be considered, after which it will be rewritten by a seasoned scriptwriter anyway and you will lose all control of it.

. . .

NONE OF THIS, which we have discussed almost as much as the plot itself, interests Kevin, who I see is now back on all fours, standing square in the middle of the blanket like a tiny, long horse, brimming with energy. No, not energy; outrage. Outrage, I imagine, either at me for having brought a thin and measly blanket, or at us not having done anything sufficiently diverting since we left home.

"What?"

He stares at me and starts wagging his tail. My friend turns around from the computer screen.

"Maybe he's bored."

"Maybe."

Kevin barks.

"No, no barking. We haven't finished yet. You'll just have to sit down and wait."

He huffs, readying himself for another bark.

"I said no barking. Sit down and wait. We won't be long."

He sits down on his hind legs, still outraged. But then he huffs and stands up again, looking as if he is about to bark. I raise a finger and he shuffles on his feet before sitting down on his hind legs again, albeit this time more relaxed.

We go back to our script, but our discussion about the realities of the film world has left me a little disheartened and wondering why we are making so much effort for something that will likely never see the light of day. Struggling for ideas, I shrug my shoulders and suggest that maybe the character just wanted to do what she does in the film and that's it. It doesn't need explanation.

My friend looks at me pityingly.

"No one just 'does' anything. There's always a reason, whether it's to do with themselves or someone else."

Of course I know that. I've always known that. I just can't be bothered to think. Maybe Kevin is right and it's time to stop.

I glance down at him and he's made himself as comfortable as he can on the second-rate blanket. He is still staring at me, but with hangdog eyes, as if the whole world is against him. I look away. I'm not quite ready to give up on writing for today.

"Okay then," I say. "Why? Why does she do it?"

We launch back into it and explore what we've sketched about her character and past to see why she would choose to betray her father.

"She mustn't feel loved," I suggest. "Maybe she never felt loved. Maybe she is so grateful to this new guy for making her finally feel wanted, even though he's only acting that way because he wants to use her, that she'll do anything for him. And if it means punishing her father in the process, then all to the good."

My friend doesn't look convinced. "Maybe. But don't people who have been wronged by their parents just try harder to win their love, rather than take revenge?"

I have to admit that I don't have a suitable answer to that, other than to suggest that perhaps he is her stepfather. As I say it out loud, I realise that I am trying to make the back story fit the plot, rather than creating living, breathing characters and letting them drive the story forward. She clearly isn't sufficiently well drawn and we don't know enough about where she has come from and what she would do in the present. After all, none of us can change the past; it's what we do in the present that counts. But we are nevertheless products of our past and have been moulded by it.

We look at each other for a minute, trying to think

of a way out of the impasse. Then my friend tells me about a video on YouTube and we decide, rather conveniently, that the business of the day is concluded.

KEVIN IS STILL WAITING on his blanket, lying down but sighing and with his eyes wide open, ready to spring into action the moment we decide to do something interesting. As I gaze at him, someone who Kevin ran up to earlier pops his head around the door and suggests we go to the pub. We check the time: 5.30pm. Are we going to get any more work done today? Probably not. We could just go now. It's not too early for the pub. And it is Friday, after all.

Kevin has been watching the conversation out of the corner of his eye, his eyebrows waggling as he switches his gaze from one speaker to the other and back again. When I say, "Okay, let's go," he starts wagging his tail, but doesn't move.

"Do you want to come, Kevin?"

He gets up and stretches himself, drawing out his head, then his neck and his body, splaying out his front legs and the toes of his forepaws, dipping his back all the way to the floor like a cat, and then moving to his hind legs and toes, before stretching out every last inch of his tail. He shakes his fur back into place and stands in the middle of his blanket, wagging his tail. He is not outraged this time, but content, and ready.

I clip on his lead and pull the blanket out from under his feet, then get ready myself. He looks confused when I tell him to wait in the office with my friend while I go to the loo, and bounces around like an excited horse when I come back and put on my jacket. The colleague appears in the hallway and we leave, Kevin throwing himself down the corridor, then down the stairs and into the outside world.

CHAPTER EIGHT

KEVIN CLATTERS HEADLONG DOWN THE PAVEMENT, weaving his way through the endless rivers of rush-hour people heading in 1,000 different directions. All the while, we are talking loudly and making jokes, discussing this and that and what so-and-so did, although my eye is always on him, making sure he doesn't get himself entangled with his lead or dart across the road.

We reach a pub. We haven't decided where to go and someone suggests we have a pint here while we think about what to do. He stops, splayed against the ground, but pulls himself upright and trots happily over, his tail and head up, when he sees we are going in a pub. He then puts his head as close to the ground as possible to pick up on the innumerable smells that issue from within.

While we order, he stands patiently on the floor between us, watching our faces intently. When we take our pints, he thinks we are leaving and darts for the door, but I lock his lead and pull him back towards us. He gives up on leaving and trots back to resume his spot in between us, looking from one face to another as, between sips of beer, we throw jests and comments back and forth.

Pint follows pint and eventually he sits on the floor, patiently waiting and looking around the pub. A passing barmaid takes a shine to him and asks who's he is. He is so gorgeous, she says, so well behaved. Of course I have to say not always, at which point he stands up and wags his tail. I'll bring him some water, she says, and leaves. I know what's coming next, but it seems churlish to refuse. It would be needlessly disappointing, although she will be disappointed anyway.

We go back to our conversation, laughing at some stupid situation none of us will remember later. The barmaid returns with a bowl brimming with water. Kevin gets up and ambles over, wagging his tail. When he sees what it is, he sniffs the water, looks up at me, and then turns away. I knew he would never drink it. I don't know why he drinks only water I give him and dirty rain puddles, but he invariably refuses everything else.

Undeterred, she pulls a couple of treats out of her pocket. They always keep a jar by the bar for when customers bring in a lovely little doggie, she says. I smile. She proffers one to Kevin and he steps forward. He delicately sniffs it, gives it a little lick, and then backs away. She tries the other one and he is even less interested. They both look up at me, him as if he wants me to get him out of this awkward situation, her with pleading disappointment in her eyes.

"I'm sorry. He's very picky about what he eats. He doesn't seem to like most treats."

I wonder if I have one of his old favourite treats in my pocket for her to give him, but I stopped giving them to him months, even years, ago and I doubt he remembers them.

"Sorry," I repeat.

She smiles at him and gives him a rub on his ear. "Never mind, it's probably better for your health anyway." She stands up, adjusts her clothes and smiles at me. "It's nice to meet you."

"Nice to meet you too."

She lingers for a moment, smiling, then leaves. My friend is staring at me, smirking.

"Does that always happen?"

"What?"

"Barmaids coming up to you and asking to give the dog a treat."

"Oh, yes, everywhere we go."

"And you didn't even try to pull her?"

"Um, what? No, of course not. Why?"

"You're crazy."

"What do you mean?"

"She didn't just come over to say hello to the dog."

"No?"

"No. She came over to chat to you. The dog was just an excuse."

I look down at Kevin. He is staring at me with an expression that seems to say, 'What next?' I reflect for a moment on how many women have come up to me in the last week to talk to me about Kevin and wonder how many it would make if only five per cent were interested in me too.

"Really? You think so? You think some of them are interested in more than just the dog?"

"Obviously. How many guys come up to you to talk about the dog?"

"Hmm, only a few. They're usually gay."

"Exactly. He's an ice breaker. People feel like they can approach you because of the dog."

"Oh, right. You don't think it's just because women and gay men are more interested in dogs than straight men?"

"No, of course not. Dog loving is not gender-related. Hey, you couldn't lend me Kevin, could you? I'd score loads of girls with him."

I look down at Kevin, who is happily wagging his tail.

"Don't listen to him," I say, and then turn back to my friend. "No way. He's not a tool for 'scoring' girls, and anyway, if anyone is going to be scoring anything thanks to Kevin, it's going to be me."

"How's that ever going to happen if you don't even realise it's going on?"

I look across at the barmaid. She is dealing with other customers and laughing. I wonder.

"She's not my type."

"Christ. Does it matter? You don't have to marry her. Just go out with her for a week or two, have some fun and then forget all about it. You don't have to be soulmates."

I gaze at her again, and then turn away when she looks in my direction. I look down at the dog. He is getting impatient and bored. He wags his tail when he sees I'm looking at him. I am strangely proud that he doesn't take treats, as if he is a dog with good taste. She did try to give him one of those cheap ones, and I don't think he's had one of those since just after I got him.

His taste has changed drastically over the years, and I have drastically changed what I give him. When I first knew him, he got traditional tinned dog food, until I realised how it was made and that dogs shouldn't eat meat all the time. I gave him treats then too, but most of them had only the most tenuous of connections with real food. I slowly phased them out, swapping them for his chew sticks and switching him to dry food.

For many years, he had trouble with holding in urine and always seemed to be a little bit ill. Sometimes, I would go to dinner parties and have him on my lap if I couldn't be bothered to bring a bed. When I got up, I would find he had urinated all over my legs. It was embarrassing, but I worried more for his health. He would sometimes wee in his bed or on the sofa, always when asleep. I took him to vets and read articles online. He had numerous tests and examinations and all sorts of theories were put forward.

Eventually I read or was told that a simple change in diet could be enough to help him. So I sought out organic largely vegetable-based dried food handmade in London. Within a couple of weeks, his life was transformed. Not only did he never wee himself again, but his coat became shiny, he got a spring in his step and he seemed years younger. His muscles bulked out and he became fitter and stronger. And his temperament changed. He calmed down and was much easier to live with.

And then he started refusing almost all other food.

"SHALL we finish these pints and go on?"

I look up at my friend. "Down in one?"

Without another word, we all down the remainder of our pints and, taking his cue, Kevin launches himself towards the outside world.

As I leave, I glance back and see the barmaid. She looks up, smiles and waves. I wonder for a second, and then remember I am terrible at chatting people up. It would have all been so much easier if my friends hadn't been there.

CHAPTER NINE

THE STREET AGAIN, AND THE HEADLONG DASH. I WONDER
if Kevin is hungry as he lunges for a piece of cold pizza
on the corner of Goodge Street and Charlotte Street. I
pull him away just in time and he spins across the pavement, hardly missing a beat before carrying on down
the road, full of determination.

My friend laughs and asks if Kevin is always like
that. Is he? No, of course not. But put him in a busy
street plump with possibilities for stolen treats and
tasty discoveries, and he turns, like Dr Jekyll, into his
Mr Hyde, driven to drunken madness on the intoxi-
cating smells. It can be irritating, funny and puzzling,
all at the same time. But what must it be like for him to
be so overcome? I imagine it would make him perfect
for hunting in the woods or across an open field. His
utter fixation on smells would be beneficial, even es-
sential, there. If you were hunting, that is.

The closest I got to seeing him in hunting mode,
rather than blindly chasing after dropped food and rot-
ting carrion, was when we were living in a rather second-rate flat in a third-rate part of town, rented from a
decidedly fourth-rate estate agent. The rule was clear:
no pets. But the landlord almost never visited the flats,

lest they should discover jobs to do, and so we lived in tranquillity in our downtrodden nest with no disturbances.

Out of the blue, the landlord announced they wanted to visit for an annual check. Curious that, given it was the first time in almost four years that they had got around to making an annual check, but who was I to argue? The immediate and most pressing realisation was that there could be no evidence of the dog when they made the visit, which was due in a couple of days' time. Fortunately, we were friendly with the neighbour upstairs, who rented her place from a different agent and had a different landlord, and so I arranged to take Kevin and his ever-growing collection of toys and paraphernalia upstairs.

When the time came, I was running late and fretting somewhat over the idea that the landlord might arrive early and catch us out, mid-changeover. I rushed upstairs with the dog and his bed, and told Kevin, who by this time had a very confused look on his face, to wait while I got the rest of his things. He wagged his tail and then, as I went to leave, looked behind me and dived under the neighbour's sofa, scrabbling on her wooden floor.

I didn't have the time to wait and see what he was up to, so ran downstairs to fetch the next batch of things. By the time I made it back upstairs, he was waiting for me on the landing, wagging his tail, with what looked like one of his toys in his mouth. Funny, I didn't remember him having a small grey toy, and anyway, I hadn't started bringing them up yet. As I got closer, he excitedly stepped forward and dropped what I realised was a mouse at my feet.

"Oh, well done."

He sat back on his haunches with a look about him that suggested he was very pleased with himself. I put down the overstuffed bag I was carrying and inspected the mouse. I was horrified to discover that, despite a punctured rib cage and obviously broken hip, it was wasn't dead, but panting heavily and rather desperate.

I checked the time. The landlord was due in fifteen minutes. I had to act fast, and the mouse needed to be put out of its misery. But what could I do? And with what? I glanced around the open-plan living room and kitchen, while Kevin watched me with intense expectation.

Spying a cereal bowl on the draining board, I grabbed it and weighed it in my hand. It was solid enough. I crouched down over the mouse and checked it again. Still alive, still suffering. Kevin was standing right next to me, watching the proceedings with great interest, his nose by my face. I pushed him back and raised the cereal bowl over my head. I caught Kevin's eyes, glistening and wide with anticipation, and hoped the poor mouse wouldn't suffer too much. I swung the bowl down and hit its head.

The bowl bounced off the mouse's head and... the poor thing winced from the pain, but was still very much alive. I looked at Kevin.

"Dammit."

He looked down at the mouse, and then back up at me with an expression of 'now what?'

"I'll have to do it again, but harder this time."

Kevin looked down at the mouse, and then stepped back. Without waiting, and praying I got it right this time, I swung the bowl over my head, and then down as hard as I could. There was a thud and a sickening crack, and I knew it was all over. When I lifted up the bowl, the mouse was clearly dead.

I picked it up with some kitchen roll and dropped it into the bin by the sink. As quickly as I could, I brought the rest of Kevin's stuff upstairs, leaving him standing at the top of the stairs, wagging his tail, but with a rather puzzled look on his face. I then settled down to work in our flat as if nothing was amiss, waiting for the visit.

Hours later, when Kevin and I were on the sofa, me watching a comedy and him dozing gently, I heard our neighbour come home. *I must thank her. She helped me so much today.* Unable to drag myself off the sofa, however, I decided I'd do it tomorrow and stroked Kevin.

Seconds later, a scream filled the house. I wondered what had happened. Then it hit me.

"Oh God, the mouse. I left it in the bin, uncovered."

Kevin opened his eyes, looked up at me, then went to sleep.

OUT IN THE ENCROACHING EVENING, we reach Goodge Street station and stand around, deciding where to go, Kevin glancing from person to person, shivering slightly. Finally we head into the station and down the escalator.

"Do you always carry him like that?"

I look down at Kevin, nestled comfortably in my arms as we head down into the Tube.

"You have to. There's a sticker at the top and bottom of every escalator saying that dogs have to be carried."

I shift him in my arms and he watches the people ascending on the other side.

"What, even people with big dogs?"

"I guess so."

"What a pain."

"You don't often see people with big dogs on the Tube, although I have seen someone carrying an Alsatian up the escalator."

We all laugh at the idea and are still talking about the issues of having a dog in central London when we get on to the Northern Line. There's plenty of space around the doors, so I put Kevin down in the middle of the floor and he splays out his legs. All the while looking me in the eye, he sways with the rocking of the carriages, like an underground dog-surfer. I don't hold on to anything either, and we sway together, our friends laughing at us.

Maybe it is a little strange, but it's one of those things we do when we're together and in our own world. He is a little self-conscious as a performer, but he doesn't seem to mind people staring at us too much. Unlike Bessie, my father's old dog.

When they were on their own, my father would sing with her while she howled, but she wouldn't do it when anyone else was present. When I was staying with him, he put her on the kitchen table and they got ready to sing. He started, but when it came to her turn, she kept looking at me out of the corner of her eye and wouldn't do more than the smallest yelp.

I SMILE at Kevin as he sways on the floor in front of me. Not for the first time, and probably not for the last, I wish I could talk to him: have an actual conversation and understand what he really thinks and feels. When we first went on the Tube, he panicked and tried to bolt every time the door opened, but now he seems to enjoy it, not only for the chance to underground dog-surf, but also because he likes watching people and them coming over to say hello.

As we roll into the station, he wags his tail and walks up to me. He jumps up against my legs, asking to be picked up. I oblige. I always do.

CHAPTER TEN

THE DAY HAS DESCENDED INTO EVENING BY THE TIME WE reach Old Street and the bustle of Shoreditch. The sunset is spread across the sky, framing the ramshackle collection of houses, shops, hotels, flats, offices and workshops with purple gold. I pick him up again. There are too many people and too many things to scavenge to let him roam free.

When people notice I am carrying a dog at their eye height, they are mostly delighted, captivated by his open, curious attitude and his deep eyes. He always looks slightly worried in these situations and that, mixed with his inquisitiveness, makes him look intriguing, charming and beautiful, all rolled into one. People smile, or laugh, or make a comment, sometimes to him, sometimes to me, sometimes to the world at large. Most people who see him can't help but react.

On Hoxton Square, I drop him to the ground and he happily trots along. The square is filled with artists, Trustafarians, office workers, drunks and the homeless, all cheek by jowl on a small patch of grass surrounded by galleries, bars, offices, restaurants and, incongruously but hinting at the more prosaic side of the area, a primary school.

Now, in the gloaming, the square hovers, no longer a daytime escape from the constant noise and movement of Old Street, and not yet the scene of myriad evening stories, fuelled by the supercharged electricity of alcohol and drugs, driving life to excess. The revellers, young and old, are still gathering, arriving from their working week and slowly slipping into their night-stalker selves, chasing dreams that seem closer now, yet remain always out of reach, never quite to be captured in the clear reality that lies just outside the bubble of intoxication. Intoxication? On what? Who knows? Life? Maybe.

We, friends, are seeking a night out, wanting to empty our minds and let in possibility. Down a side road, I spot a luxury coach, maybe one of the many that bring revellers down to Shoreditch from Birmingham and other far-flung cities so they can rub shoulders with hedonists they read about in magazines and create stories to tell their friends and family back home. We aren't sure what to do. After a few drinks and the enforced pause of the Tube journey, we are hungry. Maybe we could be sensible for a change and eat before we continue drinking.

We find a place in the corner of the square. The staff won't let us in, on account of the dog, but they say we can eat on the terrace outside. We regard the sky, now falling blues and greys, and decide it's just warm enough. We can always zip up our jackets to our chins and order in more drinks to ward off the cold.

I put Kevin on my lap and he gratefully drapes himself across my legs. I remember it's past his feeding time and he must be thirsty and hungry. Asking the waitress for a bowl of water, I give him the carrot and chew stick I have in my bag.

"Sorry, it's all I've got," I say when he polishes them off and comes back for more. It's not enough and I feel guilty, but I can't do much about it. The shops in the neighbouring streets will only sell dog food in tins, and that wet, processed meat makes him ill. The waitress brings the bowl with an indulgent smile. I offer it to Kevin and he gratefully slurps down the whole lot.

We order and I take Kevin back on my lap. Still feeling guilty, I break a dry bread roll into small pieces and surreptitiously feed him it while we are waiting for our order. He gobbles it down greedily, all the while staring up at me.

My friends and I wander through story after story as the wine flows and we make our way through dinner. I recall a time when I and one of our merry band ate at the same restaurant maybe a year before, also with Kevin. The waitress – the same one who serves us now, although she doesn't remember us – assumed we were a gay couple having an evening out with our pet dog. She didn't say as much, but it was obvious from the way she spoke to us and smiled at Kevin, and then back at us, as if he was our child.

The waitress is under no such illusions this time, not least because Kevin is tired and makes no attempt to take part, not even to beg for food, but also because my friends are being loud and boisterous. It has been a while since I have been out, and it is good to be back in the world and enjoying life.

I have been much more lucky in finding work of late, and have had enough to get over the worst of my financial difficulties and set myself straight. Just to know that we can go out and I don't have to think about how much things cost or ask if we can skip dinner is a relief after months of hanging back, refusing invitations, choosing carefully and trying not to make it obvious that I am in straitened circumstances.

This is the other side of being freelance, of course, and I am relieved to be able to live again. Although I must remember I will have taxes to pay and it may not be the end of the lean times for good. When you work from one small short-term job to the next, there can be no let-up. You have to do everything to the maximum at all times. I have got used to that rhythm and, when I had no work, not having it made me feel useless and wretched. Work coming in makes me feel wanted, needed even, and gives me a reason to carry on, to be positive and engaged with the world around me. Of course, Kevin has been a constant throughout the lean period and, in his own way, encouraged me to keep going.

One morning, before work picked up and I could start to live again, I woke up and stared at the ceiling. I was at the end of the road. I couldn't carry on. I had just five pounds to last me the week and there was precious little hope that I could find any work, let alone be paid, anytime soon. How would I cover my rent? How would I eat? I had enough food for Kevin until the end of the month, but what then? And with no work to do, what would I do all week? I tried to make some calculations, but nothing made sense. I didn't know what to do, and would have panicked if I hadn't been crushed by the weight of it all. I wondered if I had the strength to cry, but instead I just stared at the cracks in the plaster.

This is it. There is nothing left to say or do.

My hand was hanging out of bed as I lay prostrate, waiting for some sort of divine force to take me away.

This is then the end. There is no way out.

After a few moments, Kevin pushed up from his bed and placed his head into my palm. He moved his head from side to side so that I was stroking him, although I wasn't doing anything. Involuntarily, I smiled and looked down at him. He wagged his tail and stretched from the tip of his nose to the end of his tail. Walking over to the bedroom door, he stared at the handle, and then back at me.

Time to go for a walk. Time to get up and go outside. Time to keep going, not to give up.

We walked outside and along the cut to Greenwich Park. London had never looked so glorious in the autumn sunlight, and Kevin skipped happily in the grass, looking back every now and again to check I was still coming.

WE PAY the bill and wonder aloud what we should do next after our satisfying meal. The night is yet young.

"There's a nightclub just over there," one of us says, pointing vaguely at the nearby buildings.

"Where?"

"Just two doors down. I went there last week. It's small, but pretty good."

"But how on earth would we get in? We've got a dog with us."

"Don't worry about that," I say.

CHAPTER ELEVEN

I DON'T KNOW WHY I AM SO CONFIDENT WE'LL GET INTO the club. Kevin walks happily alongside me as we leave the restaurant, and all I can think of is how brilliant it would be to have him in there with us.

As we arrive, I see there is a short queue and two bouncers on the door, who look the serious no-nonsense and definitely no backchat types.

"What are we going to do?"

"Don't worry, you can't see what you aren't expecting," I reply blithely.

My friends look at me as if I am mad, but I pick up the dog and hold him at hip height, balancing him on the point of his ribcage so he almost hangs there. I sweep my jacket over his back and he hooks his hind paws on to my trouser waistband and belt to steady himself. They stare at me, incredulous that I think it'll be okay, as Kevin's head is sticking out of my jacket, plain for all to see, and his front paws are dangling down in front of me. I smile winningly and we join the queue.

When we get to the front, one of us is frisked by a bouncer, which makes me hold my breath. But despite that, and the time it takes for us to have a chat with the bouncers, during which I am standing close enough for Kevin, should he have desired, to lean over and touch or sniff at least one of them, they don't notice that a dog is suspended in mid-air by my waist.

After what seems like minutes, they wave us in with a 'Have a good night, lads'.

Inside, we laugh, amazed that we got away with bringing a dog into a nightclub. We then look around and realise that it may not be that great a venue. I wonder about the loudness of the music, which is ear splitting, but I remember that dogs hear sounds in a completely different way to humans. Kevin often sleeps by the speakers at home, sometimes with his head resting on the soft foam, even if I am playing music at a volume that, to me, seems almost unbearable.

I lift him properly into my arms and check him. He is completely unfazed by the experience and totally at ease.

Looking around again, I realise that it's great that we got him in, but what, exactly, are we going to do with him now that we are inside? I certainly can't put him on the floor, as I have no desire to accidentally in-duce a scene from a cheap farce, and I can't very well dance with him in my arms. I tried that at a friend's birthday party, but it was a sort of mini festival in the woods and we danced among the trees. He could go to bed whenever he wanted there. But here? Well, there don't seem to be too many options, and I don't want to get even more hot and sweaty than I would otherwise be by holding a dog while I dance.

We find booths with seats at waist height in a corner and I drape Kevin's blanket over one of them. When I place him on the seat, which is in a slippery faux leather, he immediately lies down and looks rather content. We decide to take it in turns to watch over him. At first, I feel guilty at imposing that on my friends, but they don't mind and, anyway, we can't dance all the time, one of them says. We all need a break from time to time. And it's too damn noisy to be able to talk, so what's the point in us all staying together all the time?

The first time I head off to the bar and dancefloor, I look back all the time at our friend sipping his rum and coke and people-watching, and Kevin lying in a semi-circle on his blanket, his nose tucked into his paws. I wonder again whether it's all such a good idea and I shouldn't just go home and put Kevin, and myself, to bed.

When I return to the booth, I find another one of our number happily sitting next to the dog, stroking him while sipping his cocktail and looking around the dancefloor. He hops off his seat and heads into the mêlée while I take my turn dog sitting. I am rather pleased to spend some time to one side, taking everyone in and watching the flirting and the dirty dancing. I can see why my friends have been content to hang back for a while.

As I am watching from the sidelines, I think, not for the first time, that I am rather grateful to have the dog with me on a night out. His presence – his need for care and to be taken safely home in one piece – puts a natural brake on my excess and keeps me within the limits of, if not exactly sobriety, then at least propriety.

I used to drift too easily into drinking too much, becoming drunk and blacking out. There were so many times I woke up at home, unsure initially where I was, unsure of how I got home and of how the evening ended. So many times I texted my friends the next morning to ask what happened after so-and-so point, nervous they would tell me that I behaved appallingly or, worse, not reply at all, so offended were they at my behaviour.

I have established that I am, by and large, a happy and congenial drunk who seeks to do no harm and cause no offence. Nevertheless, in my darker times, when I felt hopeless and lost, I sometimes acted in a way that I didn't recognise as being me. Of course it was me. I did those things, as people made clear, but they were not at all how I would want to behave or, in any other circumstances, would be capable of behaving.

We can all behaving appallingly, given the right, or wrong, circumstances. This is hardly new. And we all must spend our lives ensuring that we act in the best way possible, whenever we can. What shocked me was that, at times, there was no end to the depth of my self-loathing and, if I got drunk in those periods, I lashed out at the universe and said and did things that could be hurtful to people. I don't mean anything criminal, but I showed anger to people I love, and it made me ashamed, especially when 'I' wasn't really there. There was evidently a subconscious version of myself that was a wounded animal, fighting to keep people away so it could lick its wounds in private.

With Kevin, I cannot get so drunk that I become insensible or have blackouts. I must observe the limits and it is a relief to know that I will always be okay and the person I want to be when he is around. I have noticed before now that I feel a little useless when I do not have something or someone to care for. It is why I initially wanted to be a doctor, and it manifests itself in a strong desire to do service to other people or to my country, or to look after and nurture the vulnerable. Sometimes I wonder what that says about me. Does it describe a lack in me, a hole that needs filling?

I didn't really understand it until I met Kevin and slowly came to the realisation that looking after him and seeing him develop and express himself with me makes me feel fulfilled in a profound manner. It gives me a satisfaction that I have not experienced before. Will that be even greater when I have a child?

ONE OF OUR group leaves the dancefloor to have a break and take over dog duties for a while. I am slightly disappointed. I was enjoying stroking Kevin while watching the drinkers and the dancers and their night games. But I don't want to stay watching forever.

I thank my friend and ask him what he would like to drink. A rum and coke. I'll make that two. I check the dog is still sleeping, or at least pretending to. He looks so calm and still, as if we were at home, him lying on the sofa while I work. I don't want to leave him, but then the DJ plays a song I love. I head back into the crowd, swaying to the beat as I make my way to the bar.

CHAPTER TWELVE

OUTSIDE, THE STREET HAS BECOME A PLAYGROUND FOR the intoxicated. They are spilling out of the bars and clubs, and there are people, people, people everywhere, stumbling, strutting, laughing, arguing, running, flirting, drinking, pissing, vomiting, singing and dancing. It's Hogarth in the 21st century, complete with the homeless and the vulnerable and the pickpockets watching on from the shadows.

I leave my friends at the entrance to the club. Again, the bouncers don't notice the dog at my hip, even though his slightly bemused face is plain to see. I put him on the floor and walk down the square to Old Street. As I turn on to the main road, I instantly regret having gone that way.

A group of kids, none more than 18 years of age, all happy, drunk, flush with life and optimism, see Kevin and immediately scream with delight. They want to get down on the ground to speak to him and pet him, but I can see he is very wary of them. I pick him up and hold him in my arms. They pet and fawn over him and talk all at the same time. They proclaim undying love and wish they had a dachshund waiting for them at home. They ask the usual questions about how we cope living in the city, and I give the usual response that it's fine, because he's a lazy sofa-loving layabout. They laugh, knowing it's not true, or at least only partially.

When I first experienced this kind of reception to Kevin, I didn't know what to do or how to react. I am by nature shy and withdrawn, and prefer to slip by in the shadows. An observer, not a participant in life, or at least that is how I like to characterise it. But that could never continue with Kevin. He is a star, a celebrity everywhere he goes. He inspires obsessive, extravagant love in complete strangers; it is only their level of drunkenness that determines the degree to which it is expressed. And when people meet a star, they expect a show, something to be reflected back at them. If I try to pull him away, they are disappointed.

A star is not its own property, it is public property, which carries with it expectations and obligations. I find it hard to reconcile that Kevin is treated in this way, when he never chose any of it. He is beautiful, charming, and there is something adorable in his perfect mixture of brimming confidence and deep vulnerability that makes him oh-so compelling to be around. But he doesn't know any of that. He is a dog, usually on a mission, and he wants to get on with his things. At the beginning, I felt a need to protect him, to shield him from this attention and expectation, thinking that it was as onerous for him as it would have been for me. But I eventually accepted that, just as he doesn't know why people fuss over him so much, so he doesn't care.

He likes the attention, the strokes, the adoration, the potential for treats, and with my holding him in my arms, he never feels threatened. He takes it for what it is – people enjoying him and his presence, and their kindness and love in expressing it – so I have developed a set of stock responses to people's questions, telling them what they want to hear. They love the idea that he is silly, sometimes naughty, but always kind and generally a very good boy. They want to know he is a mirror for the kind of dog they would love to have, if only they could.

A while ago, it occurred to me that some things, some people, seem to exist in the public conscious-ness simply to bring joy into the world, and Kevin is evidently one of those. Everywhere he goes, he is treated like a movie star. He is fêted and fawned over and showered with attention and affection. I used to joke that, being with him, I had a sense of what it must be like to be Tom Cruise's bodyguard. Always there, but never at the centre of attention and barely noticed.

The difference between him and a movie star is that no one envies Kevin or wants to see him knocked off his pedestal and brought down a peg or two. He couldn't really do anything to tarnish his reputation or ruin himself in other's eyes, short of attacking a child, of which he could not be less capable.

With children, it is as if he understands their limita-tions and comprehends that they know not what they do. At a gathering on Clapham Common for someone's birthday, I didn't know many people there, maybe not even the birthday person, so Kevin and I lounged in the grass, basking in the warmth of the summer sun, en-joying the moment without fully understanding what was going on around us.

There was a baby there, seven or eight months old, who crawled over to Kevin, fascinated by this myste-rious black-and-tan creature that looked somewhat like a soft toy, but most certainly was not. Kevin lay there perfectly still and calm while she mauled his face and ears and nose, before using him to pull herself upright. I wanted to drag Kevin away, but he was so clearly not perturbed by the baby. He indulged her, let her get away with things that he would never tolerate from another living creature.

It was only when she pulled at one of his eyelids, which looked as if it hurt him quite considerably, that he simply got up and walked over to me. The baby naturally fell over, and it was at that point that I realised everyone at the party had been watching, fascinated by the calm that Kevin had shown. They laughed at his response to the final insult, which seemed to say, 'You may be able to poke me in the eye, but you can't walk, so the last laugh is on you'.

Although he was always patient and indulgent around children, he was not above using their limitations against them. When I had a cleaner at a former flat, she one day brought around her niece as the young girl wanted so much to meet Kevin after all the lovely things she had heard about him. This did not surprise me one bit. Each week, after the cleaner had finished, the flat would fall silent for long periods before she came to say goodbye and talk about anything we needed to discuss. One day, I decided to investigate and ambled out into the hallway to find her and Kevin cuddling together on the floor.

When she brought around her niece, she was very happy to introduce her to the famous little dog, and he was sweetness itself. He sat down very nicely in front of her, and I asked the young girl whether she wanted to give Kevin a treat. Of course she was delighted with the idea, although we had to stop her automatically putting the breakfast kibble I gave her in her own mouth. Laughing at her mistake, she stretched out her hand and he carefully and gently took the kibble and ate it.

The cleaner asked her niece if she would like something herself. Kevin immediately sat down expectantly again, which made me smile, but I thought nothing of it. The cleaner handed her niece a piece of chocolate and, clearly miffed that there was nothing for him, Kevin sprang up and jumped at the girl. He pushed her in the chest and, as she fell back, she threw the chocolate up in the air. Turning expertly from his lunge, Kevin grabbed it in mid-air and ran down the hall, eating it before he reached the end and before I could stop him. The young girl was shocked and a little shaken, and I apologised profusely, although inside I was impressed at his ingenuity.

I LEAVE the excitable group on Old Street and wander down the road, still carrying Kevin in my arms. Fewer people notice him that way, but when they do, they are just as effusive as the youngsters. I spot my favourite bagel place, tucked into the corner with Curtain Road, and decide to stop off. I'm not that hungry, but these bagels are the best, and I love the tiny kitchen and counter, taking up the smallest possible space between two buildings.

There is a queue, but I'm not in a hurry. I stand and watch the drunken crowds, slightly amazed to see them, as I suppose when I lived there in another time in my life, I was one of the revellers.

A young lad from Liverpool is just ahead of me in the queue and he tells me my dog is lovely. I've been so lost in people watching that I have almost forgotten that I am carrying Kevin. I thank him. He asks me how long I've had him and I can see he wants to talk, and not about the dog. Ooh well, it's a long time now, I tell him. Maybe eight or nine years. He asks me the usual question about how it is to live in the city with a dog and I tell him it's fine. But how is it for *him* to live in the city? He tells me it's okay, good even, but he misses home. It's harder to fit in here than he thought it would be. He has a good job and the money isn't bad, but it's very expensive and the people aren't as friendly as in Liverpool.

I know how he feels. Living in London sometimes seems little more than an exercise in spinning plates, and it can be very trying to have to make so much effort simply to keep everything turning. And he's right, the people aren't as friendly, if you compare it with Liverpool or, say, Leeds. But you have to pick the right places to go. You have to find your London, your people, your places, your hangouts, your refuges, and you have to get away from time to time, otherwise it can become claustrophobic and even oppressive. It can be hard to keep your head above water, but you can if you focus on what's important to you and don't get distracted by the noise.

He wonders if having a dog would help him feel more settled, but then he says that he works in an office and couldn't get home early enough, let alone at lunchtimes, to take the dog for a walk. I tell him that was one of the reasons I went freelance, because I could see that Kevin was lonely during the daytime, and that was while I was living close enough to work to be able to pop home and take him out during the day.

By now, we have got our bagels and are eating them on the street corner. Kevin stands by my feet, looking up, ever hopeful. The Liverpool lad and I watch the revellers for a few moments, and then say goodbye. I watch him trudge down Curtain Road, and then I turn towards home. Realising we're off, Kevin scuttles in front of me, searching for whatever he can find.

CHAPTER THIRTEEN

To keep our journey home quiet and avoid the crowds, we take the back streets. Away from the rowdiness of Shoreditch, the roads are almost empty and otherworldly under the streetlights. There is scarcely any traffic and only the odd pedestrian, and it is like a film set. Every now and again we see another dog walker in the distance or the disappearing tail of a fox.

Over the distant hum of the city, a scooter starts up and is driven away. We turn a corner and see a group of people discussing something very loudly, as if there is no one else in the world. Somewhere, something heavy falls, although it is impossible to say what or where.

Kevin glances up at me. He is happy trotting down the street, barely taking an interest in his surroundings, but firmly leading me home. He knows the way. We must have walked these streets 100 times and, although we are well over a mile from home, he knows every road and byway. He even seems to know that the parks are closed at night as he doesn't head for them as he would during the daytime, but walks around them, glancing through the railings from time to time. Or maybe he believes that it is quicker to walk the streets. He ignores the bins and the dropped food, ploughing on and on, taking us closer to our beds. He is focused. He must be very tired.

I am relaxed and happy. We've had a fun evening and I wasn't – actually, no one was too drunk. I look up at the tops of the buildings. The streetlight forces me to see things differently. Some windows in the nearby block of flats are illuminated, but most are not. How many lives? How many sleeping? I think of the Liverpudlian and wonder how long he will stay in London. I guess only a few months more.

I listen to the tippety-tap of Kevin's claws on the pavement. His pads, after a day out in the city and barely a chance for grass beneath his feet, will be hot and dry. He will sleep well tonight. I listen to my own echoes as I trudge along. I am tired. I will sleep well tonight too.

We round a corner and I spot a movement out of the corner of my eye. Before I can register what it is, I know it's danger. I use Kevin's harness to spin him away from it and pull him up into my arms in one fluid movement. An American bull terrier, millimetres from catching Kevin in its powerful jaws, slides to a halt under my arms. I can feel Kevin shaking through my jacket. Knowing it has missed its chance, the terrier walks off, all the while regarding Kevin out of the corner of its eye.

Its owner appears from around a corner. He is middle aged and well dressed – I have seen him driving his classic car around the neighbourhood.

"Why the hell did it go after my dog?"

"Oh, sorry. I didn't see it. I was back there."

"But why would it do it? Why would it attack my dog?"

"I don't know. Maybe she thought he was a rat."

Offended on Kevin's behalf by the insult and mystified as to how the man thinks a full-size black-and-tan dachshund could possibly be mistaken for a rat, I walk away, still carrying Kevin in case the terrier decides to have another go. As we head down the road, we both constantly check over my shoulder. Why is it that Kevin is so often attacked by other dogs?

"No wonder you always go for the kill first," I say as I finally put him down and he runs towards home.

I remember an episode a few years earlier when a Staffordshire bull terrier appeared from nowhere out of the driving rain and grabbed Kevin by the head. Realising he was seconds away from being killed, I slapped the terrier on the arse as hard as I could, and it, thankfully, let go. Its owner tried to tell me off for hitting his dog, which was almost amusing in its ridiculousness, although it was only later that I saw Kevin had two puncture marks in his head, clearly made by the dog's teeth as it tried to crush his skull.

So many incidents. A beautiful greyhound called Alfie tried to chase Kevin down somewhere in Islington and just missed him, only because I picked Kevin up in time. Alfie had a killer glint in his eye that day that left me shaken.

Maybe it's no surprise that Kevin has a difficult relationship with other dogs. When we first got him, his former owners emphasised on the phone that they wanted rid of him because he couldn't get on with their other dogs. When we got there, we found a small house that stank of dog urine, a vastly overweight man with a deathly grey pallor, his much younger, nervous wife in a pink tracksuit and with greasy hair, and three obviously untrained young dogs. The man, who was only interested in our money, told me that they wanted to get rid of Kevin, as I named him on the train home, not just because he didn't get on with dogs, but also because he was okay when he was young, but now he pulled too much on the lead. The wife chipped in to explain that her husband had already had three heart attacks and it was all getting too much for him.

Kevin couldn't wait to leave that house with us and bolted down the street towards the station. He was curious and intrigued to be out in the world, and I thought that he would simply be happy to be away from that terrible place. He was happy, at first, but he soon found it a struggle to adjust to his new life.

Little did I know that he had never been for a walk, so he had no muscles and was very unfit. The wife had let slip that he had only ever been let out into their backyard to do his business and had never gone out for a wee, with the result being that he simply pissed in his bed. He didn't even know how to cock his leg. I tried to show him by example late one night by cocking my own leg against a lamppost, at which point he gave me the most confused look I have ever seen on an animal.

He also had scars in his fur, which was one step away from being mangy, and he was very afraid. Afraid of the doorbell, of loud noises, of anything being raised towards him. I realised how bad his life had been when I lifted up my foot to check my laces while going downstairs. He squealed and cowered in the corner. The fear in his eyes broke my heart and I decided I would give him as much love as I could and encourage him to express himself as fully as possible. I never wanted to see him cower in fear and mistrust again.

I recall that the grey man's wife said the other two dogs had made life difficult for Kevin. It makes me angry at what he suffered, and guilty that I never reported the couple to the RSPCA.

His adjustment to a 'normal' life was a long, hard process. I had never really believed in the concept of animal mental illness before I met Kevin, but it quickly became apparent that he was severely depressed. I would guess that, in the end, it took him more than two years to get over the trauma of the first one-and-a-half years of his life. But once he did, he flowered.

The overweight grey man had told me that Kevin had been the runt of a litter from a championship winning pair of dogs. That, he said, was why he was a bit small, why his back wasn't as straight as a standard dachshund's, and why his eyes were so big. The man had seen those things only in terms of their value; they made Kevin less valuable and, as a consequence, undesirable. But I, and most of the rest of the world, saw that those differences made him all the more special and, in the end, more beautiful.

Maybe all those instances when he was attacked, and his terrible upbringing, explained why he was so aggressive with other dogs. Maybe to a degree, but not entirely. Why did he bite an Italian greyhound on the nose at a friend's party, for instance, when it was obvious that this tiny, gentle dog simply wanted to say hello? Why did he plant his paws on the side of a Labrador when we were lazing in a park not long after we'd got him, then reach under and bite his testicles, when the bigger dog had done nothing? How could that be justified?

WE REACH our door and Kevin waits excitedly, staring at the lock, and then at me, all the while wagging his tail. I know he will race inside, have a drink from his bowl, and then scamper down the hall and fling himself on the floor so that I can clean his paws. Then he will trot along the hall to the bedroom, happy and ready to go to sleep.

"At least no one can say you're boring," I say and turn the key in the lock.

PART III
BESIDE THE SEASIDE

CHAPTER FOURTEEN

ONE MORNING A YEAR OR TWO LATER, I AM AWAKE. I stare at the ceiling for a moment. I am listening to his tail swishing against his bed as he wags it furiously. He is excited. I can tell even without looking. I know he must be staring at me, waiting for me to wake up. I savour this moment before we spring into action and start the day. He will know I am awake – he watches me relentlessly – and he will become impatient if I don't get up soon, or at least look at him.

I turn and his big brown eyes are there. As I look straight at him, he wags his tail even harder and licks his lips.

"Morning."

He shuffles slightly on his bed.

"How are you today?"

He leans his head to one side. He steps forward slightly and I realise he can't decide whether he wants me to stroke him or take him outside.

"Do you know, we have nothing to do today?"

Still wagging, still staring.

"It's the weekend. Well, it's Friday and I don't have any work today, and I've nothing planned for the weekend."

Can that be true? I ponder for a minute. Do I really have nothing arranged? I think through my friends. Everyone is either away or busy.

"We could do something, just the two of us."

But what? We've done so much in London. Almost everything you can do with a dog, in fact. And I don't feel like doing anything with anyone else. Just him and me.

"We could go away for the weekend."

I stare at him and he dips his head and licks his lips. He is still wagging his tail.

"But where? That is the question."

Where indeed? If we go away for the weekend, I don't want to see my family or friends outside of London. So that rules out heading north. I don't want to spend too long travelling. Not only is it tough on Kevin to spend too long on the road, but also I don't feel in the mood. And I don't want to drive. What does that mean? No more than an hour and a half on the train, and it has to be somewhere interesting and, ideally, unknown.

"How about the seaside?"

He stops wagging his tail. He doesn't know the word, I'm sure, but I remember trying to get him to walk on the beach at Brighton and him refusing to step on the pebbles, which were just the right, or wrong, size to slip in between the pads on his paws. That and the time we went to Holkham beach, where he nearly fried in the heat.

"Hmm, not that. Let's find somewhere on the coast you might like. No pebbles. It's October, so it won't be too hot. And somewhere with plenty to see."

One-and-a-half hours away and on the coast. That means south or east of London. Not too east and not Brighton, for aforementioned reasons. I look at the map on my phone, scrolling along the blue. Worthing, no. Rye, no. We've been there. I start again in Kent. Margate? Too far. What about Whitstable? No, we've been there too. I scroll back and forth.

Hold on, what's that? Eastbourne? I try to think of anything I know about it, but nothing springs to mind. I look it up. The tennis tournament, but that happened months ago. What else? It seems to be a slightly old-fashioned and, to me, forgotten seaside destination. It sounds right up my street. And there's Beachy Head, with its white cliffs and whiff of wartime endeavour. Perfect.

"Shall we go to Eastbourne?"

He is lying down on his bed, no longer wagging his tail. He is staring up at me imploringly, with his head on his paws.

"Hold on, we need somewhere to stay."

I search for dog-friendly B&Bs, finding a whole host of sites I never imagined existed.

"Maybe lots of owners take their dogs on romantic getaways."

And there it is, a B&B not far from the sea, not too far from the station. From the pictures, it looks perfect in its faded glory, like it was made for us. But how will we get there? I check the trains. There's a direct service leaving from Waterloo station in two hours.

"I think we can make that."

I glance at the dog. He's either hungry or needs to go for a wee. I've been a little selfish doing all this and not attending to him first.

"Hold on, give me two minutes."

He knows 'two minutes' and immediately stands up again on his forepaws and starts wagging his tail, swishing it against his bed.

I quickly book the B&B and the train tickets, and then leap out of bed. He runs around after me, putting his nose on my feet with every step, begging me not to leave him behind.

"If I could explain what we're about to do, you would be so excited. I really wish I could tell you in a way you would understand."

I pull on his harness and slip on a coat, watching him stare into my eyes and wag his tail as I do it up.

"It's a shame we have to go out now for your morning ablutions. We could save quite a bit of time if you could wait. But how can I convince you to wait for something you don't know is coming?" I smile at him and hold his head in my hands. "You're going to love it."

He had stopped wagging his tail, but he starts again and, as I open the door, he bursts through and flings himself headlong down the stairs.

When we get back, he watches me nervously out of the corner of his eye while he quickly chews his breakfast, knowing that something is happening and desperate not to be left out. I march around the house, trying to think of all the things we will need. I pack scattergun, placing a bag on the bed for me, adding things as I think of them, before breaking off to do some of his packing, bit by bit, as I think of things for him.

At some point, he runs around in a frenzy because he sees me tipping out his food into a plastic bag and tying it up. He barks at me, standing stock still on all fours in the middle of the hall, his tail quivering with bristling tension.

"It's okay, you're coming with me. I wouldn't bother doing all this and then not take you with me."

He is unmoved.

"Look," I say, throwing down his harness and lead in the middle of the floor, "you're coming with me."

He steps forward and sniffs at it suspiciously. He then runs after me as I march back into the bedroom to pack the next thing that pops into my head.

Eventually, I am showered and ready, and looking at what I have assembled. Enough clothing for me for two days, plus an iPad, a notebook and my Bronica medium format camera. I think about taking a 35mm, but I know the pictures won't be as good. It's a pity the Bronica is so heavy, but it's always worth the effort.

Then I check his things. A coat, a rug for when he's on my lap, his food, chew sticks, a water bottle, a couple of carrots for the journey, wet wipes, collapsible water and food bowls, and his favourite blanket. I stare at his bed. I know I should take it. He has two bagel-shaped beds and he loves them, but they are so bulky and cumbersome to carry. I cannot imagine taking one, and all the rest of our stuff, with us on the train. I decide we'll be better without.

He sees me staring at the bed. He glances at it, and then back at me. I feel a little guilty at the possibility that I am being lazy in not taking it. No, I decide, we don't need it. He'll be fine. We'll manage.

"Right, let's go."

I put Kevin in his harness, grab his lead, the bags and my camera. He skeeters down the stairs in front of me and I'm glad I don't also have the bed to carry. I look at him, so happy to be out in the world. He'll be fine without it.

CHAPTER FIFTEEN

THE B&B IS JUST AS I HAD HOPED, AND THE OWNER IS charming and very welcoming. The place is as old fashioned as I could have wished it to be. It's as if the outside world, with its modern conveniences and fast pace, has only partially filtered through to this quiet corner of England. There is the breakfast room and there is the guest lounge, complete with board games, books and old magazines. Of course, we will never use them, but just to know they are there is comforting. I wish I had thought of doing something like this sooner.

We are given a room right at the top of the house and it occurs to me it is in case the dog makes a lot of noise during the night. If only the owner knew how near-silent Kevin is most of the time, communicating more with his eyes and body language than he ever does with his voice. The room is small, but perfectly fine. It is a garret room, under the eaves at the top of three flights of stairs. I remember a 19th century novel and think about chocolate being heated in a pot on the stove. The room is carpeted to within an inch of its life, and the air is thick and heavy. I am tired and I cursorily unpack and drop Kevin's blanket on the floor in a pile. We both settle down and I fall into a deep sleep.

. . .

WHEN I WAKE, I have no idea how long I have slept, but it is already dark. I check the clock and it feels uncommonly early to be night time, but then again it is mid-October and the nights are drawing in. And that means that, although it was warm today, it will be very cold tonight. I've brought a coat for Kevin, but only one, and I curse myself for not having checked the forecast and assuming the weather would be like it is in central London.

No matter – I'll feed him now, and then leave him in the room while I go for dinner. He certainly won't need a long walk, if he needs one at all after the journey across town to get to the station and the trek to the B&B once we got here. So I pull myself up, still groggy from the nap, and put out a bowl of food, which he greedily gobbles down, taking mouthfuls of kibbles and flinging them on to the carpet before frantically wolfing them down with barely a chew. I watch him. I am a tad guilty that he is doing that on the B&B carpet, but then I remember that we have traipsed in as much on our shoes as he is putting down now.

I put out a bowl of water and he takes slurps in between mouthfuls of food. He must have been very hungry and thirsty. Once he has finished eating, he stands next to the bowl and stares at me expectantly, wagging his tail.

"What? Are you still hungry?"

He licks his lips and wags his tail a little harder.

"Hmm." I look around. "I can't give you any more kibbles because I only brought enough for two break-fasts and dinners."

He is still staring at me.

"Oh, I know."

I fish around in his bag for the box of chew sticks.

For some reason, I've brought extra of those, so can give him one now. I proffer one to him, but he looks doubtful.

"It's okay, you can have it."

He sniffs it, wraps his mouth around it, but then backs away.

"Look, I know you only have these in the morning, but you can make an exception if you're still hungry."

He looks up at me, still doubtful. I gave him one on the train from London and he knows he only has one a day. He almost never asks for one, except after the morning walk, and certainly never a second one.

"Go on. Take it if you're hungry," I say, wishing I'd brought some radish or cucumber. Or we hadn't finished the carrots on the way down.

He steps forward and gingerly takes the chew stick. He takes it away and lays it down on the carpet and stares at it. He sniffs it, and then decides he will, after all, eat it, working along it from one end as if he's eating a stick of rock.

"There you go. That's better."

He looks at me out of the corner of his eye, slightly unsure. Once he's finished, I take him out for a quick walk around the block. It's been raining and the ground is cold and wet. As I suspected, he doesn't want to go for a long ramble and soon rushes back, dodging the puddles and the overhanging leaves from hedges – anything that might make him even slightly wet. I am happy I brought at least one coat with me.

Back in the room, I get ready to go out again and he watches me, a puzzled expression on his face.

"You're going to stay here, while I go out for dinner."

He cocks his head on one side.

"I won't be long. I'll leave the TV on for you while I'm out, so you won't feel alone."

I turn the telly on and find the BBC. The news is showing.

"There you go, something informative. You can tell me all about world events when I get back."

He doesn't look at all convinced. I go over to his blanket and arrange it for him, him watching me all the while. I lift up a corner and invite him to go inside and settle down.

"Come on, in you go."

He looks at the blanket forlornly, and then up at me.

"Come on."

He reluctantly ambles over and sits on his hind legs underneath the piece of blanket I am holding up. I drop it over him and he looks ridiculous, half-standing under his blanket. He stares up at me sadly.

"I won't be long. You'll be all right."

He stares at me.

"Okay, well, I've got to go, otherwise I'll be late back."

I put on my coat and he looks at me with indignation.

"I'll be back. Promise."

I step towards the door and he barks and lunges at my feet.

"No."

He tries to bite my laces and undo them.

"No. Go to your basket."

I feel a bit silly calling the rather pathetic arrangement a basket, but that's the command he knows. He reluctantly pads over to his blanket and sits on top of it.

"You'll be okay. I'll be back soon."

He stares at me.

"Stay."

Still staring.

I go to the door and he doesn't move. I go out on to the landing and close the door. Silence. I take one step down the creaky stairs and he is at the door, barking and yelping. I go back up and open the door in time to see him run back to his blanket and sit on it, wagging his tail.

"I said 'stay'. I'll be back."

He watches me as I close the door. Silence. I take one step down the stairs. Silence. Another one. Silence. A third and he is at the door, barking and yelping. I know it's never going to work but I try again anyway. I go back up and open the door. He is sitting on his blanket, wagging his tail.

"Stay."

I close the door and don't make it four steps down the stairs before he is barking and yelping. I climb back up the stairs and open the door.

"Okay, you win. You can come with me."

CHAPTER SIXTEEN

OUTSIDE, IT'S COLD, BRACING IN THE SEA BREEZE. AND the ground is wet, very wet in places. He is in his coat, but he is not at all happy about the wet ground. He walks with small steps to avoid flicking too much water up on to his belly and he glances up at me reproachfully as he dodges the puddles and drips from trees and hedges.

We walk along the seafront. It's bleak on a wet and cold October evening. I see a restaurant across the road. It looks warm and welcoming, but certainly not the kind of place that would take dogs. I feel sad and a little regretful that I can't have my cosy and leisurely dinner in a nice restaurant, perhaps reading a book or writing some notes as I while away the hours.

I look down at him and he glances up at me as he forges ahead, returning his attention firmly to the ground to find the driest path through this horrible wetscape. Yes, it would be lovely to be in a cosy restaurant enjoying my own company, but we are here in Eastbourne together and that, as they say, is that. I wanted to go on holiday with Kevin, so what would be the point of having regrets over not being able to do something without him?

"You're a good boy."

IN THE FIRST few days after he arrived in my life, he was quiet and obviously relieved to be in a new place, but once the anxiety and depression set in, it consumed him totally and he was extremely difficult to live with. Whenever the doorbell rang, he would launch into frantic barking and yelping as if he was about to be tortured. He would scratch and struggle, and try to savage anything or anyone that came through the door. Postman, neighbour or friend, it made no difference. He would attack them all, pulling at their clothes and barking ferociously as if his life depended on it. He could not be reassured or calmed down, until he finally accepted after several minutes that the 'intruder' was okay and not to be dismembered on the doorstep.

It reached the point that any disturbance, any hint that the perfect tranquillity of our home was to be threatened, would pitch him into an existential panic that was awful to watch, and doubtless awful to experience. Worse, he rarely remembered anyone from one time to the next, which added a layer of social embarrassment, regardless of the fact that, once calm had been restored, he was beautifully affectionate.

Eventually we bought a high-pitched alarm that, when pressed, would emit a loud, piercing noise at a frequency audible only to dogs and put them off doing whatever they were doing. The idea, I suppose, was to generate an anti-Pavlovian response. Barking and yelping at the door would become associated with a negative consequence – the alarm – and he would stop doing it.

It worked, at first. There were, however, two issues with the alarm that I had not anticipated. I don't know what it says about me, but I could hear the alarm almost as clearly as he could, which was not only irritating for me, but also added to the stress of the moment. The second problem was that Kevin quickly learned to ignore the alarm and went back to barking and yelping, albeit wincing every time I pressed the button.

And then, one day, without any warning, he stopped becoming frantic when the doorbell rang and largely ignored it. Just like that.

AS WE WALK along the seafront in Eastbourne, I recall another cold evening, or so it was in my memory of it, a few weeks after we got him. It could have been any time, although it is always 9pm in my recollection of it. In the part of London we lived, there are many streetlights and they are left on all night.

It had become apparent that Kevin was extremely agitated when we went out for walks, I suppose because he had never really been on them before, despite now being over one-and-a-half years old. So we always made sure he was secure on the lead, especially when we went to the nearby park, a place that would have been full of homeless people and drug addicts every night had it not been so brightly lit.

We walked around as usual that night, nothing different, but either we hadn't done his collar up properly or he had lost weight again, as he slipped out of his collar and ran.

We panicked and ran after him, shouting for him to stop and come back. He thought this was a wonderful game and ran all around the park and into parts we had never visited. He would stop, watch us get close, and then run off again, further and further away.

Finally I realised that he was never going to come back if I didn't change my tactics. I stopped shouting for him, but instead told him he was a good boy and everything was okay. He stopped running and let me get within six feet of him. Kevin and I stood watching each other like cowboys in a Western. He was observing me very closely, ready to run at a second's notice. What should I do? I had no idea. The seconds ticked by, and still we regarded each other, me not daring to advance.

Then I remembered he liked playing with my keys. I took them slowly out of my pocket and showed them to him. He watched me and looked at my hand. I threw them into the space between us. He stepped forward to sniff them and I stepped forward too, reaching down to put his collar back on. He didn't move, leaving his head down so I could attach him more easily. Once he was secure, I picked him up and held him close, realising in that instant just how much he meant to me.

WE ARE STILL STROLLING along the windswept seafront at Eastbourne, and I am beginning to despair. I am hungry and tired. I want just to eat and get the evening over with. It's raining again, albeit lightly, and Kevin looks up at me with his well-worn 'what on earth are we doing?' expression. I have to admit that I have no idea. We have walked far from the B&B and nothing has seemed remotely suitable.

As we reach the pier, I see people standing around the entrance and, as if by magic, a fish and chip kiosk appears, one that is mercifully open. Relieved, I take my usual order of haddock and chips with a pickled egg. Finally, everything seems to be falling into place and any sense of regret at the way the evening was panning out was premature.

It is only when I have taken the warm parcel from the server that I see that the problem of an evening out with Kevin in cold and windy Eastbourne has not really been solved simply because I have something to eat in my hand. The kiosk is just that. It has no tables and chairs. I look around, wondering what to do. Kevin is watching me intently, doubtless hoping we will go back to the B&B. But I don't want our room to smell of fish and chips. Besides, in this weather, they'll be cold by the time we get back.

I cast around again, looking for inspiration, but realise that there is no choice. I'll just have to eat the fish and chips right here on the cold and windy seafront, with the rain holding for now but threatening a deluge at any moment.

I find the driest looking bench and sit on that, Kevin standing on the ground beside me, staring at me incredulously. The fish and chips are good, very good, and as my hunger abates I start to relax. I am now slightly more at ease with the holiday and whether or not it was a good idea. It is still cold and bleak, but I'm watching the sea roll back and forth, the waves drawing away the tension of life piece by piece.

Kevin is getting cold, though. And he must be very wet. I glance down at him and he stares back imploringly.

"I'm sorry, I can't pick you up until I've finished eating."

I show him the fish and chips and he licks his lips and stands up straight, his eyes fixed on the food.

"No, you can't have any."

He glances at me, and then back to the fish and chips.

"I know you love fish skins in batter, but you also know what happened when we went to Brighton. I gave you the skins then and you had terrible diarrhoea the next day. It was disgusting. We're not going through that again."

He grasps that I'm not going to give him any, although he evidently has no idea why.

"If only you'd remember what makes you ill, you'd be a much happier dog."

He returns to his forlorn expression and I wonder whether it was less perturbing when he was simply begging. I eat up as quickly as I can, staring at the rolling sea and trying to ignore the worsening rain.

CHAPTER SEVENTEEN

Back at the B&B, he scampers up the stairs as quickly as he can, sometimes beaching himself on the steps, huffing and puffing all the way. He is desperate to get out of his coat and be warm and dry. I hope he doesn't disturb the other guests staying in the B&B as he clatters about and scrambles on the carpet.

He bursts into the room and stands in the middle of the floor, his feet splayed, panting and staring at me with wild eyes.

"Hold on, I need to get your towel," I say as I take my coat off.

He looks as if he could leap at me at any second, which I sincerely hope he does not, as he is surely completely filthy.

I grab a towel from our bag and throw it on the floor. He walks into it and sits down on his hind legs, already much calmer. I take off his dirty coat and he bows his head, eyes turned up towards me. I fling it through the bathroom door and into the bath, and then rub him thoroughly with the towel. He was cold and very wet, that much is obvious. As I clean between the pads on his paws, he leans to one side and gently slides to the floor, leaving him half-wrapped in the towel while I carry on.

"Is that better?"

Once I'm done, I stop and he lies there in the towel, gazing back at me contentedly. I smile at him and rub his back.

"All over now."

I gaze at him a little while longer, and then get to my feet. He flips his body like a mackerel on the deck of a boat and lands on his feet, staring at me, fully alert.

"Don't worry, I'm not going anywhere. We're staying here for the night."

I take off my shoes and he relaxes. He wanders around the room, inspecting everything. He takes a drink and checks inside his food bowl, then trots over to me and sits on his blanket.

What's the time? Only 10pm? I'm very tired. I think about going to a pub, if I can find one I like. But that would mean either trying to leave him again or taking him with me, with all that entails. What would I do with him while I was there? Normally it would be fine, but he would end up dirty and wet again, and he wouldn't tolerate being left on the floor in that state, not in a pub. In addition to which, going to the pub would mean me getting my coat and shoes on again and facing the bracing weather, and I am not inclined to make the effort for unknown rewards.

Whenever do I go to bed early and simply read? Almost never. Maybe tonight's the night.

I think of tomorrow. The forecast says the weather should be nice, but how reliable is a forecast in England, especially in October? I hope the weather will be at least better than today. Being outdoors with Kevin when it's windy, cold and wet can be intolerable if he isn't in the mood. It's one thing if we are at home, with all our things around us and plenty to do if we want to cocoon ourselves from the weather. But here? In this cramped room at the top of a B&B in Eastbourne? I think again of the guest lounge, full of long shadows when we came back from our fish-and-chip excursion, but it won't be suitable for hanging out for long periods with a dog who has a need to explore new environments and stick his nose into everything.

I regard Kevin, who is sitting on his blanket, staring blankly at the television in the corner of the room, and hope for both our sakes it will be a nice day tomorrow. It will bring what it brings, I decide, happy in the end to have an early night with my book.

"Let's get plenty of sleep, eh? We've got a big day ahead tomorrow."

He glances at me, looking rather unimpressed by our adventure so far. I laugh and he looks at me properly.

"We're going to have fun tomorrow. We're going to explore."

No response.

I get ready for bed. When I am about to get between the covers, I notice that Kevin is still in the same position, sitting on his hind legs on top of his blanket, staring into the middle distance. I know what the problem is immediately, but I pretend to ignore it.

"Come on, time to go to bed."

I step over to him and he gets off the blanket and stands in the middle of the floor, staring at it. I arrange the blanket nicely, folding it so that there is a pocket for him to step into, and hold up the end like a tent.

"In you go, time for bed."

He looks at me incredulously.

"Come on, get in your basket."

Same expression.

I lower the fold of the blanket. "Look, I didn't bring

your bed and I'm sorry. It's not the same sleeping on the floor, I know, but it is your favourite blanket."

It's not. That's the red alpaca one a friend brought back from Peru, which he obsesses over, so much so that I have to put it away most of the time. But this one is his second favourite by far.

I lift up the flap of the blanket again.

"Come on, get in your basket."

Kevin slowly lifts himself off his hind legs, stretches, and then reluctantly walks over. He takes one step under the flap of blanket, and then turns and faces me, staring at me.

"Lie down, there's a good boy."

Slowly he lowers himself on to his hind legs and sits.

"Lie down."

He lowers himself down and I drop the blanket over him.

"You see, it's not so bad. You'll be fine."

He stares at me coldly. I get into bed and read my book. After a couple of chapters, I become sleepy. I glance across at Kevin. He is exactly as I left him. He has not made himself comfortable or settled down to sleep, just lain where I told him. I decide to ignore the obvious.

"Goodnight, Kev. Sleep well."

I stroke his head, but he doesn't respond. I turn out the light and wait for him to sigh and lick his lips, but he doesn't and I fall asleep.

AT AN UNKNOWN HOUR OF DARKNESS, I am awake. I have no idea why. I was dreaming about…

There's a soft bark and I know why I am awake. I glance across at Kevin. He is standing in the middle of the floor, staring at me intently.

"What? What is it?"

He stares at me, and then at the floor. I look across and see his blanket is a jumbled mess. He can't untangle it enough for him to be able to sleep in it. He must have been flinging it about in frustration and has decided that I need to sort it out.

"Look, I'm sorry I forgot your bed, but you'll have to sleep in the blanket. It's all we've got."

Without getting out of bed, I reach over and shake out his blanket. I half fold it and hold open a flap for him to get in. He wags his tail and walks over, slotting himself into the gap and then turning around so he is facing out.

"Good boy."

At first he sits on his hind legs, but eventually he lies down.

"Good boy. Go to sleep now."

I turn off the light and stroke his head. Still no sigh nor lick of the lips.

CHAPTER EIGHTEEN

I WAKE UP TO FIND THE WORLD ENTIRELY CHANGED. Gone are the grey clouds, the wind and the rain. In their place is a perfect pale-blue sky, and the sun is shining brightly. Kevin is lying half under his blanket, watching me calmly as I get out of bed. I smile at him.

"There, that's better. A brand new day."

No response, but his face is peaceful. I hope he slept.

"We're going to go out there." I point at the window and he follows my finger. "We're going on an adventure."

His expression remains unchanged.

"But first, breakfast."

I get dressed and we head out for a quick tour around the block. The drying streets are alive with light and it already feels warm.

"Not cold today, eh?"

He glances up at me as he navigates his way via the driest areas of the pavement. His walk is determined and focused. He's going to have a lot of energy today.

Back in our room, he wolfs down his breakfast while I get ready. When I go downstairs to get my own breakfast, he sits calmly on his blanket and doesn't make a sound when I leave. I nevertheless spend my time over breakfast worrying that he's barking and whining at the door of our room and waking up the other guests. I finish quicker than I would have done otherwise and race back upstairs, only to find him peacefully lying on his blanket, clearly having done nothing at all since I left.

While I was having breakfast, I asked the B&B owner where would be good to go on a long walk with a dog on such a glorious day. He told me the path up to Beachy Head starts at the end of the promenade and we could spend the whole day exploring the cliffs, if we wanted. So I pack Kevin's water bottle, some snacks and a blanket, taking my iPad and a notebook just in case, and my camera.

HE TROTS HAPPILY along the promenade and I am amazed at how little we had noticed of Eastbourne when we had been along there the night before, the bad weather forcing down our eyes and our spirits. We begin the ascent to Beachy Head, Kevin revelling in running on the grass. I decide I have been a little pessimistic in bringing a jacket and a hat with me when the weather is so evidently good and not about to change. He stares at me impatiently while I rearrange myself, but in doing so I spot a shack selling sandwiches. I buy lunch and a coffee, half of which I spill on our way up the hillside due to the vibrations from the lead as Kevin bounds through the grass.

As we near the top, I start taking pictures, which means he has to wait. He stands, staring at me until I put the cap back on the lens. When we finally arrive at the top, I am astounded at the landscape, which stretches into the far distance.

As it has been such an impromptu trip, I've had no time to do any proper research. Consequently I have no idea what to expect. I try to read the plaques recounting the history of the place and its role in the Second World War, but Kevin keeps pulling me on, jerking the lead to continue. I can always read them on the way back. He'll be tired by then.

I turn and stare at him. His legs are splayed against the grass so I can't pull him back and his neck is stretching as far as it will go in the direction he wants to follow. It reminds me of a trip we had to Cornwall a few years before.

We stayed in a B&B then too, one with its own brewery, and we spent hours exploring the clifftop paths. There, the path was forced to follow the ups and downs of the jagged rock formations, and passed from time to time perilously close to the edge. Kevin, being low to the ground and extremely agile, is more like a mountain goat in these situations than a dog, albeit one that becomes lost in the pursuit of interesting odours. I, on the other hand, remain resolutely human in my abilities.

At one rather tricky point along an eroded section of the path, he spotted, or thought he'd spotted, something partway down the cliff. Without any warning, he pitched over the side and dived headlong for a hole several feet below the edge. My instinct, honed after so many years on the hazard-filled streets of London, is to lock his lead to stop him going any further. But the violence and angle of his descent was such that I lost my footing and was pulled over with him. It was only by grabbing a handful of thankfully well-rooted grass that I managed to stop myself from falling on to the rocks below.

After I had steadied myself and rather unfairly admonished a bewildered Kevin, I imagined what would have happened if I had fallen. I would have ended up taking Kevin with me. While I was sure I would have died on impact, I was equally sure that he would have survived and become stuck down there, no one knowing we were there and no one, even those at the B&B, knowing we had even gone out for a walk.

The thought of Kevin being stuck made me feel awful, no matter that I would have died, and I told him to be more careful when we go along clifftops in future. How ridiculous. It's I who should be paying attention.

ON BEACHY HEAD, we walk on and on, following the well-worn footpaths that criss-cross the cliffs. We are in another world, away from London, away from everything. Kevin is so happy to be out in the sunshine, running on the soft grass.

Not for the first time, I feel guilty about living in the city. I do my best to take him to parks and ensure he's not trapped on hard pavements, bombarded by pollution and the endless vibrations from the buses, cars, taxis and the Underground passing beneath the streets. But even with the parks, it is not a natural environment for a dog like him. He is a hunter and one that wants to hunt in the countryside with his owner.

I am reminded of *Sketches from a Hunter's Album* by Turgenev. In another life, I am a wanderer, beholden to no one, exploring the countryside and encountering lives in the company of only my dog. There is a scene where the narrator is curled up in the hollow of a tree for the night, with his dog by his side. I try to imagine Kevin putting up with that and laugh. He stops and looks back at me.

"You wouldn't last more than five minutes under a tree without your favourite blanket and your bed."

He stares at me for a second, and then canters happily on.

· · ·

AFTER A BRIEF STOP FOR LUNCH, we walk on and on. We've been up here for hours, going further and further away from the town. At some point, I see that he is getting tired. I wonder if he will make it back to the hotel in one go and decide we should head back straight away.

I turn back and he trots happily beside me, rather than stretching off into the distance. He begins to slow down and fall behind. After another five or ten minutes of following what I think is the shortest route across the clifftops back to the B&B, he stops entirely, sitting on his hind legs and staring at me. I glance around and spot an empty park bench not too far ahead. Maybe he can sleep there.

"Come on. We'll go over there and have a rest."

I tug on the lead, but he doesn't budge. Trying again, I soon give in, pick him up and carry him to the bench. His body is hot and heavy, and he licks his lips with pleasure at being carried.

At the bench, I arrange his blanket on my lap and get out his bottle of water and my iPad. He takes a long, long drink, and then I pull him on to my lap. As I get my iPad ready to do a drawing of the scene, he falls into a deep sleep.

CHAPTER NINETEEN

AN HOUR OR SO LATER, KEVIN SLOWLY WAKES UP. THE time has passed so gently. After I'd finished my drawing and written a few notes for a project I will no doubt never finish, I simply took in the view, enjoying the warm, heavy weight of Kevin sinking into my lap. He slept so deeply that he didn't even dream one of his yelping, jerking, running dreams, his slow breathing the only indication that he was still alive.

He opens his eyes and looks up at me without moving.

"Did you sleep well? Feeling rested?"

He pricks up his ears.

"We've still got a long way to go to get back to the B&B, you know."

I take him off my lap and place him on the ground beside me. He stretches himself thoroughly, from his nose to the tip of his tail, and when he is done, he snorts and shakes himself out. Then he stands fully upright, staring straight at me, ready to go.

"Let's have a drink first."

I take a swig from my bottle and he watches me, glancing at the bottle and then at me. I know he wants some too. His bottle is empty, so I direct the flow of water from mine into my cupped hand and he drinks from it as if it was a bowl. When he has finished, he stares into the distance, his body language telling me he is thinking of doing something, but has no real desire to do it. I glance around, seeing a woman and her dog going for a walk, far enough away for us not to hear them.

"Come on, let's go back."

I clip him into his lead and we set off back to the B&B. Kevin is revived after his sleep and drink of water, but less excitable than before. He is calm, in fact, and trots along at the same speed as me, just a few feet ahead. He is on the lookout, as always, for anything that might stray into his reach, but not with any conviction or purpose. He is merely going through the motions.

We arrive at a point overlooking the town and I take it in for the first time. Instead of trying to pull me along and keep going, Kevin sits beside me while I wonder about which way we should go back.

Between our high vantage point and what I assume is the B&B, I can see a couple of sections of beach which look semi-deserted, despite it still being a lovely, warm day. Tempted by the water, although unsure whether that will stretch as far as entering it, I head with Kevin down the narrow path to the sea.

We arrive at the far end of the promenade. The sea is calm and an appealing blue, rather than the wintry grey I'd expected before we left London. Happily, the beach is more sandy than stony and I reckon Kevin won't protest too much at walking on it.

We pass the first section of beach, and then I head down to the sand. He is a little reluctant, but relents when he realises he can walk comfortably on the surface.

We make our way further down towards the sea. About half way, Kevin pulls back. He stands up straight, ears out, feet planted in the sand. He will go no further. I think about picking him up and carrying him the rest of the way, but I remember an episode from that same trip to Cornwall a few years ago.

ON ANOTHER CLIFFTOP WALK, we stumbled across a bay, perfect in its design, hidden from view and, apart from a family at the far end, entirely deserted. Eager and determined, Kevin led me down the narrowest of paths, winding around rocks and passing close to the most precipitous of falls, until we eventually spilt out on to the beach, which was a mixture of rock pools and sand. It was a perfect blue summer's day, hot but not overly. The ideal spot to enjoy the weather and the water.

With no one around other than the family, who were at least a couple of hundred yards away, and considering Kevin's lack of skill in sand walking, I was content to leave him on my towel while I messed about in the water. The only thing was that I didn't have any swimming trunks with me, but no matter. I could swim in my underwear, and then dry out in the sun.

Back on the beach and happily soaking up the rays, I watched Kevin, who was staring at me rather mournfully. True, he never really enjoyed the beach, but at least he normally found it tolerable. How could I make it better for him?

As I was putting my clothes back on, it occurred to me that it was a real shame that he had such a pathological fear of being wet and in water. Ever since I had known him, he had avoided puddles and rain, drips and any chance of getting even remotely wet. It was perhaps not surprising that I had never seen him jump into a lake, or even walk up to the water's edge. Of course, I could now bathe him without him panicking or trying to get out of the bath, but it had taken years of hassle and stressful moments to get that far. Now he simply stood there with the expression of a soldier about to face a firing squad, but at least he tolerated it.

"You really ought to try it, you know. It's wonderful to be in the sea."

He stared back at me, still mournful.

"It's only a question of becoming used to it. Look at you in the bath. You're fine doing that now." I thought for a minute. "You know what, why don't we try it now?"

I looked around. There was still no one apart from the family, who were packing to leave.

"Okay, let's go."

I got up and put on my t-shirt. Picking up Kevin, I carried him to a large, very shallow rock pool. I stepped in to test the temperature. Perfect. Like a bath or the Caribbean Sea. Even better, the water only came up to the top of my feet.

"Try this."

I put him down in the water and he stood there, rigid and unhappy, with the same off-to-the-execution expression he wears when it's bath time.

"Relax. It's not going to hurt you, and you're never going to enjoy it if you don't relax."

Nothing.

"Okay, come with me."

I bent down to pick him up and he jumped into my arms.

"I'm not giving up on you yet, you know."

I started walking towards the sea. I was holding Kevin only by his shoulders, thinking I would drop him into the water, at which point he would see that it was all okay. But the closer we got to the waves, the more I could feel his body stiffen. He was staring at the sea over his shoulder with wild eyes, as if a monster was approaching.

124

"Don't worry, it's just the sea. You'll be fine."

As I finished speaking, a big wave rolled in and, seeing it approach, Kevin lifted his bum up to get away from the water. As he did so, he urinated all over my t-shirt and boxer shorts.

I held him away from me and stared at my clothes, and then back at Kevin. At least he was looking more relaxed.

"I guess that wasn't such a good idea after all."

ON THE BEACH IN EASTBOURNE, I look at Kevin, and then at the sea. The water looks colder than it was in Cornwall and the waves are, if anything, bigger here.

"Maybe we'll just go back to the B&B, eh?"

As I start walking up the beach, Kevin makes sure I'm definitely coming before running back towards the stairs to the promenade.

CHAPTER TWENTY

Back at the B&B, he runs to his bowl and excitedly awaits his food, which he is so desperate for, he eats it straight from the bowl to start with. It is only when he is a little more sated that he takes out the kibbles and arranges them across the carpet before eating them.

While he eats, I lie down and listen to him crunching, heading back to the bowl, pausing to check for any new smells, then taking out a batch of kibbles and fanning them out. It is one of those rare moments when I am aware of the significance and simplicity of the life we share, and realise that our time together will not last for that many more years. What is he? Nine? Ten? He is in fine form, the best of his life, but he had a hard life in the beginning and, since I have had him, he has had a couple of serious illnesses that have taken their toll.

I think back to a time when I got out of the car in a square somewhere in Hoxton after several weeks away. He had stayed with neighbours, who adored him and whom he adored in return, and I knew he was waiting with them in a cafe across the other side of the square. I gave the 'I'm over here' whistle and he bolted towards me at full pelt. I crouched down and he leapt into my arms, licking my face and ears and wriggling with delight.

I do not know a purer love than that, and never will. Any relationship with a human is laced with their need, and right, to have an independent life, the implicit choice that is therefore woven into the relationship making it all the more thrilling. But an animal, especially a dog, dedicates its life to you, willingly, and to have experienced that on such a profound level with a dog so emotionally communicative and intelligent as Kevin is a privilege that I will not know again in this way in my lifetime.

He has finished eating and wanders around the room before heading to his blanket. Before he can get there, I pick him up and hold him close, kissing him on his neck and behind his ears. He turns in my arms and nibbles and licks the end of my nose. It is not my favourite of his signs of affection, but it always makes me laugh.

I pull away and look at him.

"Give me a kiss."

He licks me on the chin.

"Thank you."

I kiss him on the neck again and put him down. He ambles over to his blanket and clambers on top. I help him underneath and he turns around so that his head is sticking out, with the rest of him covered. I drink a glass of water and think about getting changed before heading out for dinner. All the while he watches me with half-closed eyes.

When I go out for dinner, he barely lifts his head. I close the door quietly and walk softly downstairs. Before I get something to eat, I catch the falling light on the seafront, the sky filled with purple and gold shells stretching off to the horizon.

I think about Kevin. When I held him just now, I

was reminded that he doesn't smell of anything. His fur, when he was pushing against my face, smelt of grass, sunshine and the sea breeze, but not of dog. When just out of the bath, his fur has the faintest canine aroma, but otherwise he takes on whatever smells there are in his surroundings. It is perfect for hunting alone with his owner, and he magnifies his ability to take on other smells when we are in the wild by eating the dung of what I assume he thinks is potential prey, although it seems somewhat ambitious to think he could go after a stag.

This lack of innate odour is lovely for a human, but does it have consequences in the rest of his life? Is this why he is so often attacked by other dogs, because he doesn't smell like another dog, or of anything at all?

I think back to *Perfume* by Patrick Süskind. Maybe he is right that if we don't have an odour, we cannot be recognised by other members of our species as 'one of us'. If so, it is a sad aspect of Kevin's life, as he has been left unable to socialise with other dogs. I have to admit that this is partly his fault, as he is often aggressive to his fellow canines. Although I suppose this could again be related to his lack of odour. After all, if he doesn't have an odour, how could he recognise the odour of other dogs as indicating they are part of his tribe?

I understand. I often don't feel part of the human race, other humans seeming somewhat alien to me. I have never really felt comfortable occupying this space, in being a person in the world. Perhaps this is what has driven us closer. If I don't feel human and he doesn't feel like a dog… well, at least we have each other.

But it begs the question: what does he think he is, and what does he think I am? Does he think he is not a dog and we are both humans? Or does he think I am a dog? I look out to sea and smile to myself. Am I, to him, a dog? Certainly I understand him better than any other creature he knows and, in some ways, he under-stands me more than any person I have ever met. And I am most comfortable when communicating with him.

Perhaps with him, I am a dog.

BACK IN THE room after dinner, I take Kevin, sleepy and compliant and half-melted in the heat of his blanket, out for a quick walk. He runs back to the B&B after the first chance to have a wee and waits eagerly for me at the door to our room.

Once I am in bed and he is again wrapped up in his blanket, I reach out my hand. He pushes his head up into my palm and I scratch the top of his head and be-hind his ears. When he lies back down, he sighs and licks his lips. He falls into a deep sleep, and so do I.

ABOUT THE AUTHOR

L. A. Davenport is an Anglo-Irish author. He sometimes lives in the countryside, far away from urban distraction, but mostly he lives in the city. He enjoys long walks, typewriters and strong black coffee.

To find out when L. A. Davenport has a new book out and get the latest updates, visit his official website at Pushing the Wave. He can also be found on Twitter.

To keep up to date with all the latest news, sign up to L. A. Davenport's official email newsletter, and receive a free short story.